# BIBLICAL INCREASE AND PROSPERITY GOD'S WAY

### *YOU WERE CREATED TO INCREASE, DOMINATE, AND MULTIPLY IN THIS LIFE!*

## (TIMOTHY R. WILLIAMS)

# Dedication

I want to thank my wife Tammy for all the sacrifices she has made over the past 47 years. I am thankful for all the times I have been away on the mission field and she never complained. All the days and hours I have been in my office, planning trips, writing curriculum, sermons and books. She was sent by God to be my soulmate and ministry partner. I have to thank my children and grandchildren for allowing me to do what God called me to do. I want to thank my brother Tony for sowing into this project and helping to make it possible.

There are many people over the years that have helped, encouraged and pushed me to get me to the place I am today. The notes in this book were taken while attending Rhema Bible Training Center, Victory Bible School and Victory World Missions School. Many of these notes were taken over the years by studying under Kenneth E. Hagin, Kenneth Copeland, Jerry Savelle, Mark Hankins and many other ministers of the Gospel. There have been many pastors, friends and Bible School teachers that have shared their time and their knowledge to help me write and accumulate the notes that make up this book on Biblical increase and prosperity.

I have to thank all the ministry partners that have sown into my life that has allowed me to travel around the world to preach and teach the Gospel. Many of those partners are still sowing today to help me accomplish God's call on my life.

# Recommendations

I came to know Missionary Timothy R. Williams through God's servant Dr. Bishop David Copeland of Revival Now International in the year 2016. I sat under the teaching of this great gift to the body of Christ, the author of Biblical Increase and Prosperity God's Way as a student at Revival Now School of Ministry. Since then I have never missed to see the man of God live, teach, demonstrate the truth and revelation written in this book. This book is reflection of Tim's practical life. He echoes the command God gave Adam in Genesis 1:28. *God blessed them, and God said unto them, Be fruitful, and multiply, and replenish the earth, and subdue it: and have dominion over the fish of the sea, and over the fowl of the air, and over every living thing that moves upon the earth.* KJV

Missionary Timothy R. Williams has written a well - balanced book on Biblical prosperity based on the Scriptures not human philosophy. Principles and wisdom captured in this book can be practiced by any believer in any continent and yield the same results. I totally agree with the authors definition of Prosperity: True prosperity is the ability to use God's power to meet the needs of humanity in every realm of life. The truth contained in the definition has completely revolutionized my mental software on prosperity. As a minister of the Gospel and theologian I highly recommend this book to all Bible students, emerging and practicing ministers of the gospel, educators, researchers, leaders and all believers who want to prosper Gods way and facilitate the gospel of our Lord Jesus Christ.

Rev. Isaac Abule: Associate Pastor, Christ Presence Ministries Trainer, Shepherds Hope Training Centre-Kenya.

Tim Williams is my best friend. We were baptized the same day many years ago. I have had the pleasure of serving on the Healing Hands International Ministries board with him since 2004. The thing that sets him apart from others is his willingness to go when and where others won't.

He has written one of the best books on prosperity because it is based on God's Word. The promises in this book are real. *"Prove Me now herewith, saith the Lord of Hosts, if I will not open you the windows of heaven, and pour you out a blessing. That there shall not be room enough to relieve it"* Malachi 3:10-12 KJV.

Buddy (Healing Hands International Ministries, Board Member)

---

As believers and followers of Christ, we all should be devoted to increasing our knowledge of how we can be equipped to live a wholesome life here until we are called home. The subject of "Prosperity" has always been a diversified teaching. Knowing what God's Word says is the clarification of understanding on this Biblical subject. Tim Williams has covered this subject in 9 chapters with scriptures covering every avenue of prosperity. He explains in simple terms what our Heavenly Father created it to be to us for the "here and now". God's Word is a revelation with power. We must KNOW The Word to walk through and stay on top of life's situations. Tim clearly walks you through God's Word on prosperity in all areas of our existence in spirit, body and soul. He helps the reader understand that God is faithful to perform His Word in all areas of our life. We highly recommend this book for any person with a desire to understand the true Biblical meaning of prosperity.

Larry and Dorcas

# FINANCIAL CONFESSION/PRAYER

Father, in the Name of Jesus, from this day forward I commit to you to read your Word, believe your Word and commit my life to a life of Biblical financial prosperity according to your Word.

As a born-again believer, I am entitled to every blessing in your Word including the Abrahamic covenant that promises me and my household increase and prosperity. Your Word says YOU give me the ability to get wealth and that you will prosper me in all that I put my hands too.

Your Word in Proverbs 10:22 says the blessing of the Lord will bring wealth without pain or toil. I confess today I am not a poor person but a rich person. I have more than enough to give into every good work. I am blessed coming and going. I am increasing in land and houses, livestock and merchandise. I am not moved by what I see but by the Word you have given to me in scripture. Your Words were spoken so they could be written, so that I could speak them and use them to increase, dominate and multiply in this life here on earth.

God, I thank you that I am blessed NOW. I know that I am in Christ, therefore everything God promised to Abraham now belongs to me also. I AM BLESSED. I am abundantly supplied to be a blessing to others. I am a tither and a generous giver. I am a dispenser of God and not evil. I am an increase agent here on this earth. Thank you for making me extremely wealthy just like you did Abraham, Isaac and Jacob.

I am not a greedy person. I am a generous person and money cannot and will not corrupt me. I give to the poor without expecting anything in return because I know that you are the one who repays me for my generosity and the charities that I give to. Because I am a tither you have promised to rebuke the devourer for me, over me and my household. You have promised to open the windows of Heaven and pour out a blessing over me and my household.

I ask for forgiveness for not being a tither and a generous person in the past. God, I commit today to being a tither now: I am all in. I have entered the room with no exits I will give to you the first and best of all my income. In return, I know the windows of Heaven are open over me and blessings and favor are being rained down on me. The devil has been rebuked and removed from my life, my family, my business and my money. My crops are in abundance, people will see and call me blessed. I thank you for being my financial partner.

God I trust you as my source, my Provider, and my paycheck writer. I no longer operate on a fixed income. I trust you as you have promised in Philippians 4:19 that you will generously fill to the full any need that I may have. That includes my finances, health and spiritual needs.

<u>I am seeking You first, Your Kingdom, Your way of doing things</u>. I know that because I seek you first you will add everything I need to me. I refuse to worry. I refuse to let fear in my life and especially my finances. GOD I DO TRUST YOU.

Father, I thank you in advance that my debts are paid off, my house is paid off. All my needs and my families  needs are met with nothing lacking.

Father, I am thanking you and remind you of your Word in 2 Corinthians 9:8 where you promised that all grace, favor and earthly blessing is coming to me right now. I know that no matter the circumstances, whatever the need, I will be supplied. I refuse to fear and I put my trust in You.

**AMEN**

# BIBLICAL PROSPERITY



## Scriptures

**All Scripture unless otherwise noted was taken from the King James Version of the Bible.**

# Introduction:

The contents of this book have taken 29 years to accumulate. As you read and study this book, you will began to realize the importance of what God's Word teaches you and me about having increase in our lives. It is God's plan to prosper and bless all of His children. Many people believe we will be blessed when we get to heaven. That is correct, but The Word says He wants to bless you and me, and prosper us in this life. We don't have to wait until we have toiled and worked our whole lives to live a prosperous good life. Every Bible principle in this book is backed up with Bible scriptures. In many cases the teachings in this book will go against what you may have been told as a child. There are over 2000 Bible scriptures that relate to increase, prosperity and multiplying in this life. The world's system has taught us we must save, we must cut back, spend less in order to get ahead and prosper. You will never get rich by saving! There are many things in this life you will receive or acquire faster by sowing than saving. Do not get me wrong, we should save and plan for the future, But many people develop a poverty mentality while trying to get comfortable in this life. In this book you will receive the principles of God's written Word. This will help you break away from the broke mentality. It is up to you and me to choose in which system we will operate. Yes, we live in the world, but the Bible says we are to operate in the spiritual realm of God's system, As you study each chapter you will be challenged to make changes in what you believe. This will determine how you operate in today's world of chaos and lack. I suggest before you start reading this book you read chapter six of Matthew. Also read chapters eight and nine in Second Corinthians. May the Lord bless you as you read, learn and implement God's Words of prosperity in your life.

*KJV:* <sup>24</sup> *There is one who scatters yet increases more; And there is one who withholds more than is right, But it leads to poverty.* <sup>25</sup> *The generous soul will be made rich, And he who waters will also be watered himself.*

*NLT:* <sup>24</sup> *Give freely and become more wealthy;    be stingy and lose everything.*

<sup>25</sup> *The generous will prosper; those who refresh others will themselves be refreshed.*

*ESV:* <sup>24</sup> *One gives freely yet grows all the richer; another withholds what he should give, and only suffers want.* <sup>25</sup> *Whoever brings blessing will be enriched, and one who waters will himself be watered.*

### *2 Corinthians (9:8)*

*ASV:* <sup>8</sup> *And God is able to make all grace abound to you, so that having all sufficiency in all things at all times, you may abound in every good work.*

*NKJV:* <sup>8</sup> *And God is able to make all grace abound toward you, that you, always having all sufficiency in all things, may have an abundance for every good work.*

*NLT:* <sup>8</sup> *And God will generously provide all you need. Then you will always have everything you need, and plenty left over to share with others.*

**READ CHAPTERS 8 & 9 IN 2<sup>ND</sup> CORINTHIANS.**

**GOD IS MORE THAN ENOUGH**

**It is not Greed to want to pursue Growth.**

**This year will be a year of more. More increase, more blessings and the year of double for many.**

In this teaching on Biblical Prosperity we will discuss many aspects of finances.

In **Genesis 1:26-28** God gave some clear assignments and commands. They were not suggestions as many people believe. Let's read this scripture and then talk about what's in it. **Amplified Bible, Classic Edition**

*26 God said, Let Us [Father, Son, and Holy Spirit] make mankind in Our image, after Our likeness, and let them have* **complete authority** *over the fish of the sea, the birds of the air, the [tame] beasts, and over all of the earth, and over everything that creeps upon the earth.*

*27* **So God created man in His own image**, *in the image and likeness of God He created him; male and female He created them.*

*28 And God blessed them and said to them,* **Be fruitful, multiply, and fill the earth, and subdue it** *[using all its vast resources in the service of God and man]; and have dominion over the fish of the sea, the birds of the air, and over every living creature that moves upon the earth.*

**God said**: Be fruitful: in other words go do something productive.

**God Said**: Multiply. Many people think this is just about raising a family!

**God said**: Go fill the earth.

**God said**: Use your authority here in the earth and put it under your power.

**God said**: Rule over the earth and dominate it and everything in it.

God's plan for man from the beginning was for him/her to rule, reign and dominate, not be ruled. We are Kings and priests, it's time to stop acting like peasants or beggars. As long as we continue to see ourselves as less than we were created to be, we will always be ruled and dominated by the world system. We must realize there are two kingdoms, the worlds (Satan's) kingdom and God's Kingdom. We must make a decision, what kingdom will we choose to operate in?

**Revelation 5:10** *says He (God) made us kings and priests to our God. And we shall reign on the earth. (KJV)*

## Your results in life will never exceed the inner image of who you think you are!

If you cannot see yourself as one who rules and reigns then you never will. Many people believe the scriptures that tell us to rule and reign is for when we get to heaven. We will rule and reign with Christ in heaven. But read the scriptures for what they say. God has laid out a plan for man to live a life of increase and prosperity while he is here on this earth.

### Ephesians 2:10 Living Bible

10 *It is God himself who has made us what we are and given us new lives from Christ Jesus; and long ages ago he planned that we should spend these lives in helping others.*

**If we were created to be a king, think like a king, act like a kings, we need to know how a king should act. Let's look at several versions of the scripture in Job 22:28**

KJ21

*Thou shalt also decree a thing, and it shall be established unto thee; and the light shall shine upon thy ways.*

AMP

*"You will also decide and decree a thing, and it will be established for you; And the light [of God's favor] will shine upon your ways.*

CSB

*When you make a decision, it will be carried out, and light will shine on your ways.*



*If you decree something, it will stand; light will shine on your ways.*



*He will do whatever you ask, and life will be bright.*



*If you decide to do something, it will be successful. And your future will be very bright!*



*You will be able to do everything that you decide to do. Light from God will show you the right way to go.*



*You will decide on a matter, and it will be done for you, and light will shine on your ways.*



*Anything you decide will be done, and light will shine on [illuminate] your ways.*



*When you promise to do something, you will succeed, and light will shine on your path.*



*You will decide on a matter, and it will be established for you, and light will shine on your ways.*



*You will pronounce something to be, and He will make it*

*so; light will break out across all of your paths.*

So how does a king act? A king makes decisions, they declare things, They speak and decree things and they happen. As Spirit filled believers we are commanded in **Mark 11:22-24** to speak things into existence just as God did in Genesis. He spoke and through His speaking things were created. In the new Testament Jesus spoke and people lived, were healed and some things died. The thing we need to understand is the fact we were created in His image and His likeness.

**If you are a Spirit filled born-again believer, you are a mountain moving individual who has been given the power and authority to rule and reign as kings and priest now in this life.**

**Everything God created** that relates to man and humanity was designed to increase and multiply. We don't see increase in most people's lives and many born again Christians lives. So, the question is how and what do we need to do to bring increase into our lives?

If you ask a banker or financial advisor this question, they will tell you to save, invest and to be stingy with what you have.

The world's financial system does not work in the same way God's financial system works and the world doesn't understand how you can give instead of saving and have more!

**You will never save your way out of debt, but you can sow your way out of debt!**

# Important Financial Scriptures

## 2 Corinthians 9:6-11 & 14-15

### 3 John 1-4 Amplified Bible, Classic Edition

*1 The elderly elder [of the church addresses this letter] to the beloved (esteemed) Gaius, whom I truly love. 2 Beloved, I pray that you may prosper in every way and [that your body] may keep well, even as [I know] your soul keeps well and prospers. 3 In fact, I greatly rejoiced when [some of] the brethren from time to time arrived and spoke [so highly] of the sincerity and fidelity of your life, as indeed you do live in the Truth [the whole Gospel presents]. 4 I have no greater joy than this, to hear that my [spiritual] children are living their lives in the Truth.*

### Deut. 28:8 Bible, Classic Edition

*8 The Lord shall command the blessing upon you in your storehouse and in all that you undertake. And He will bless you in the land which the Lord your God gives you.*

### Isaiah 60:1  Amplified Bible, Classic Edition

*Arise [from the depression and prostration in which circumstances have kept you — rise to a new life]! Shine (be radiant with the glory of the Lord), for your light has come, and the glory of the Lord has risen upon you!*

### Proverbs 10:22  Amplified Bible, Classic Edition

*22 The blessing of the Lord — it makes [truly] rich, and He adds no sorrow with it [neither does toiling increase it].*

### Isaiah 52:7  Amplified Bible, Classic Edition

*7 How beautiful upon the mountains are the feet of him who brings good tidings, who publishes peace, who brings good tidings of good, who publishes salvation, who says to Zion, Your God reigns!*

## 1 Timothy 6:17-19  Amplified Bible, Classic Edition

*17 As for the rich in this world, charge them not to be proud and arrogant and contemptuous of others, nor to set their hopes on uncertain riches, but on God, Who richly and ceaselessly provides us with everything for [our] enjoyment. 18 [Charge them] to do good, to be rich in good works, to be liberal and generous of heart, ready to share [with others], 19 In this way laying up for themselves [the riches that endure forever as] a good foundation for the future, so that they may grasp that which is life indeed.*

## Isaiah 48:17  Amplified Bible, Classic Edition

*17 Thus says the Lord, your Redeemer, the Holy One of Israel: I am the Lord your God, Who teaches you to profit, Who leads you in the way that you should go.*

As believers the first thing we must do is tithe and give offerings. In other words,

### Pay God first.

**It is time, as believers we live for the maximum and not the bare necessities.  God gives us all things to enjoy. The Bible says he will give us wealth and add no sorrow to it. I refuse to settle for less than God's best.**

There is a law of progression. Do not give up. Do not settle for less than what God has planned for you.

Example: Dogs love bones. But in reality, dogs love the meat on the bones and they settle for the bone! That is the way most Christians are today about the blessing of God.

It takes just as much faith to believe for less as it does the best. You will use your faith either way.

There are three types of people in this world.

1.  Museum Keepers: They live in the past.

2.  Settlers: They will settle for anything or whatever.

3.  Pioneers: That's me and you, always stretching and looking for the best, the next assignment or adventure.

## What about tithing?

**You tithe where you are spiritually fed. This should be your local church.**

**Psalms 92:13 Amplified Bible, Classic Edition** ¹² *The [uncompromisingly] righteous shall flourish like the palm tree [be long-lived, stately, upright, useful, and fruitful]; they shall grow like a cedar in Lebanon [majestic, stable, durable, and incorruptible]. ¹³ Planted in the house of the Lord, they shall flourish in the courts of our God.*

What is the average tithe per person?

The average amount that people seem to tithe is **between 3-4%**. It is best to calculate your tithe by using the Bible as a standard. The Bible teaches a 10% tithe of your increase.

**Tithers make up only 10 to 25 percent of a normal congregation.** Eighty percent of Americans only give 2% of their income. Christians are giving at 2.5% of income.

What percentage of church goers give?

**75–90% of church members do not tithe.** The small percentage of how many people tithe is between 10–25%. Most members in an average congregation do not tithe on a regular basis.

Is tithing 10% in the New Testament?

What Does the New Testament Have to Say About Tithing? <u>**In the New Testament, tithing is less about a strict 10% and more about positioning your heart to be generous**</u>. In 2 Corinthians 9:6-10 Christians are called to generously give in response to the gospel of the Lord Jesus, based on faith in God as Provider.

What does Paul say about tithing?

In Paul's first letter to the church in Corinth, he writes, "On the first day of every week, each one of you should set aside a sum of money in keeping with his income" (1 Cor. 16:2). The church was encouraged to set aside an amount of money to give each week.

# WHO IS THE CHURCH? YOU ARE, THE BELIEVER IS THE CHURCH

## Ten Benefits of Tithing

- God is pleased by your obedience .

- God is honored by your faithfulness .

- Tithing helps to keep your priorities straight.

- You are eligible for a blessing .

- Guards Christians from selfishness.

- God loves a cheerful giver.

- Tithing supports the Great Commission.

- God will protect your stuff.

- Your possessions will flourish and prosper.

People will see your life flourishing and it will be a testimony of your beliefs.

If we go back to the Old Testament, in Deuteronomy 28, it talks about the blessing and the curse. It gives us the do's and don'ts for each.

**Note: A curse is not always something bad that happens to you. Sometimes it is something good that does not happen to you. Just because something is good, that does not mean it's a part of God's plan for you and your life.**

Being a tither will make a difference in our lives. Actually, it will change your life for the better. The Bible teaches us the benefits of tithing; my wife and I can testify to the fact it works and the blessings of the tithe is evident in our lives.

**Learn how to activate your tithing rights. START TITHING NOW!**

Becoming a tither opens doors for the believer and when you don't tithe you are subject to bringing a curse upon yourself. God doesn't put a curse on you; your disobedience opens the door to Satan and allows him opportunity in your life and finances.

The devil can keep you broke, sick and living a just-get-by life if you do not understand tithing. You must choose to participate in this blessing. I won't ever argue with a person about tithing. There are only two reason people don't tithe. One: they really have not read the scriptures and DO NOT KNOW tithing took place throughout the Bible from cover to cover. Number two: they have read it, but choose to NOT BELIEVE WHAT THEY READ and are deceived. So they don't participate and they fail by default.

God's Kingdom moves and flourishes through the tithe and the generosity of believers. I have included many scriptures in chapter nine of this book to back up what I have written.

Satan's only tool has been and still is to deceive you and keep you from acting on the Word of God. Many people believe that if they have more, increase in wealth and are blessed that somehow this makes them a greedy person. Having more wealth, money or possessions will not make you a greedy person unless you are already a greedy person.

Money is not evil; the love of money is evil which is what the scriptures say in **1 Timothy6:10**. A person who is generous when they have a little will be generous when God blesses them. But a person who is greedy with the little they have will be greedy with more.

It's the love of money that produces greed, not the money itself.

This should be the first thing we teach and preach to our children, our family, and our churches.

There is always the question "how much should I tithe." Do I tithe off my net or my gross. Do I tithe off my work salary or all the increase or income? The Bible says to tithe off the increase. **That is everything that comes into your possession that is an increase in our lives.**

God said in His Word He would bless your savings (storehouse). Just as you must decide to tithe and give God what is rightfully His, you must decide to save some for you and your family. <u>Pay God first, then yourself, then your bills and expenses</u>. (He can't bless something you don't have!) Provide a storehouse (saving account titled storehouse) so He will have something to fill and bless.

**You will learn through this series of lessons that you can actually increase through your Generosity.**

You can increase by saving the world's way and you can increase by operating by the Kingdom principles of giving. Sowing and reaping. But, saving alone will not make you rich.

**I can teach you the principles of Biblical Prosperity, but you must receive the spirit of prosperity for your life to change.**

**I WILL ENCOURAGE YOU TO SOW MORE THAN YOU SAVE!**

**Being stingy with your resources does not mean you are being a good steward with your money and resources.**

**When we are a good steward with our resources we do what Gods Kingdom principles tell us to do. "Be a generous giver."**

# YOUR SOWING WILL ALWAYS OUT-PERFORM YOUR SAVINGS

*Proverbs 10:22 says: The blessing of the Lord makes one rich, and He adds no sorrow to it.*

**Paul tells us that when you sow into God's Kingdom**

**<u>*you will have increase*</u>.**

There are many things that you have need of that you will receive faster by sowing than by saving for it.  You must have faith and believe in God's Financial System, or it will not work for you. In other words, you put action to what you are confessing and believe. We find in Scripture that Solomon was the richest man that had ever lived. He believed and practiced the generosity side of the blessing.

Lack does not come from money you do not have, it comes from money you do have and will not let go or release it. It's money you shouldn't have.

Many times, we will hold onto our money or possessions too long and it will cause us to have lack in our life.

## DO NOT LET WHAT YOU DON'T KNOW KEEP YOU FROM DOING WHAT YOU DO KNOW

**Deut. 8:18** Says; *God gives you the ability to get wealth.*

**ISAIAH 48:17** SAYS, *I AM THE Lord your God who teaches you to profit.*

**Malachi 3:8-12;** says *God will rebuke the devourer when you tithe.*

**Ecclesiastes 11:1**

**Cast your bread** *upon the waters, for you will find it after many days.* NKJ

*Give generously, for your gifts will return to you later.* NLT

This is an amazing scripture. It tells us to take what we have and sow it, wait then watch as God brings it back to us.  God will never repay you without increasing you. He is The God of increase.

Every time you give (cast your bread upon the water) you should get up every day expecting your harvest or return.

That's why we should be continually tithing, giving, and sowing. The only way you can expect something back on every wave is to continually cast and give.

To cast your bread upon the waters means to let what you have leave your control.

When you cast or let your possessions leave your control, there is an element of faith that says when you find it, when it returns to you, it will be multiplied, pressed down, shaken together, and running over. **Luke 6:37-38**

**We find three scriptures that all say the same thing. Matt. 13:12; Matt. 25:14-30** is a perfect example of Jesus saying this Himself.

**Luke 12:48,** All three say that one who has more will be given more and the one who has little, even that will be taken away. God expects you to increase with everything He supplies.

**Luke 18:24-30;** *the things which are impossible with men are possible with God.*

God will repay you for what you do or sacrifice for the Gospel of Jesus Christ.

**Ephesians 4:28;** *Let him who stole, steal no more, but let him labor with his hands so he will have something to give to those in need.*

**My harvest is not based on my need but my seed!**

**YOU HAVE TO BELIEVE AND EXPECT THE KINGDOM SYSTEM TO WORK FOR YOU.**

Your sowing or giving doesn't just affect you financially. It also affects you spiritually.

If you were needing and looking for a leader in your church, what would be the first characteristic you would look for in that person? After making sure they are saved and full of the Holy Ghost, you would want a generous person. A person who is not generous will shut down the Spirit of God and you fulfilling what God has called you to do.

## THE GOOD THING ABOUT BEING GENEROUS, ANYBODY CAN DO IT.

### Generous people will be happy people.

You need to teach these Biblical prosperity principals in your churches, not just so they will give more, but because it will open their hearts.

You teach it because it affects you and them spiritually and financially.

Some of you will get this and some of you will not. Whether you do or do not won't affect God one bit, but it will affect you!

Keep your focus on God and His purpose. He is not opposed to you being rich; He opposes you being covetous.

### You cure covetousness by being generous.

### (You should stop and repeat that at least three times out loud)

It is a great act of faith when you can release out of your hand what you are/were depending on and then sow or release it. When it leaves your hand or possession, you must begin to speak over your seed and water it continually. It is your seed and your responsibility to plant and water your seed. Then it is

God who will give the increase.

You should be concerned if you look back to last year and you were not increasing more each year.

**YOU WANT TO GROW SPIRITUALLY**

**YOU WANT TO GROW FINANCIALLY**

**YOU WANT YOUR MINISTRY TO INCREASE**

**YOUR FAITH MUST ALSO BE INCREASING**

**You must do these continually.**

**You can become rich without becoming a tightwad or stingy.**

**Remember your confession: I am a generous and cheerful, happy giver.**

**THE CHURCH IS NOT YOUR SOURCE!**

**God is your source.**

God may decide to use the church to be your supply, but many times believers look at the church as their source and not God. The Bible says God is a jealous God. I worked in the jungles of Guyana South America for seven years and then one day I heard the Holy Spirit say it is time to leave. As I began to question God about this (I did not want to leave, I loved the jungles and the Amerindian people) He said to me: These people are looking to you as their source and they are not giving me the thanks or looking to me to provide for them. It saddened me greatly to leave but in February 2010 I made my last trip to Guyana.

**Do not take and use the Words of God in vain!**

Many people think you have to use curse words to use the Lord's Name in vain. That is one way and many people do it without giving it a second thought. But you can also speak God's Words in vain. When we speak things that are contrary to His Word or when we speak but choose to not believe, we are using His Words in vain.

Example: Speaking lack, sickness and poverty over your life when the Word of God promises you the very opposite. This will hinder your blessing.

### Psalm 103:20

### Amplified Bible, Classic Edition

[20] *Bless (affectionately, gratefully praise) the Lord, you His angels, you mighty ones who do His commandments, hearkening to the voice of His word.*

**(Who puts a voice to God's written Word? You and I do!)**

**God Spoke His Word, so it could be written, so that you and I could speak it!**

**There is power in speaking God's written Words.**

### King James Version

[20] *Bless the LORD, ye his angels, that excel in strength, that do his commandments, hearkening unto the voice of his word.*

### The Message

*GOD has set his throne in heaven; he rules over us all. He's the King! So bless GOD, you angels, ready and able to fly at his bidding, quick to hear and do what he says. Bless GOD, all you armies of angels, alert to respond to whatever he wills. Bless GOD, all creatures, wherever you are everything and everyone made by GOD. And you, O my soul, bless GOD!*

# Chapter 1
# What Is Prosperity?

1 Timothy 6:9-10; 17-20

I.  Introduction

A.  **God wants us to be prosperous in every area of our lives.**

1.  This includes prosperity in our finances.

a.  Financial prosperity is neither bad nor ungodly.

b.  <u>**True prosperity is having options and choices, it means to advance, push forward, to help and succeed.**</u>

c.  **Money is not the root of evil.**

d.  It is the **love** of money that is evil (**1 Timothy 6:10** *"For the love of money is a root of all kinds of evil, for which some have strayed from the faith in their greediness and pierced themselves through with many sorrows."*)

e.  **Prosperity is not a specific amount of money.**

f.  **Money is the lowest form of power that exists on the earth. The highest form is the power of prayer.**

g.  *True financial prosperity* is having all your needs met with enough left over to give into every good work into which you desire (**2 Corinthians 9:8** *"And God is able to make all grace abound toward you,* *that you, always having all sufficiency in all things,* **may have an abundance for every good work.")**

2. Prosperity is much more than dealing with finances.

   a. It consists of spiritual prosperity, mental prosperity and physical prosperity.

   b. *3 John 2-4 "Beloved, I pray that you may prosper in all things and be in health, just as your soul prospers. 3 For I rejoiced greatly when brethren came and testified of the truth that is in you, just as you walk in the truth. 4 I have no greater joy than to hear that my children walk in truth."*

   c. You can have all the money in the world and still be poverty-stricken spiritually, mentally, and physically.

**B. True prosperity is God manifesting Himself to us in His Word. We should not judge by our feelings nor our emotions, but by what God has said in His Word.**

**C. True prosperity is the ability to use God's power to meet the needs of humanity in every realm of life.**

**II.** There are four types of prosperity. **Spirit, Soul, Financial and Physical prosperity.**

**A. Prosperity of the spirit**

1. To prosper in your spirit, you must be born again.

2. This puts you in a position to receive from God all things promised in the Word and prosper in the other areas of your life.

**B. Prosperity of the soul**

1.  To prosper in your soul, you must be able to control your mind, will and emotions.

2.  Prosperity of the mind comes when you are controlling your mind instead of your mind controlling you.

    a.  ***2 Corinthians 10:5*** *"casting down arguments and every high thing that exalts itself against the knowledge of God, bringing every thought into captivity to the obedience of Christ" (the person who does this has control of the mind)*

    b.  You cannot control the mind completely without the Word being alive and operating in you. Your mind is the only thing you really have complete control of.

3.  Prosperity of your will occurs when the Word of God controls your will. **Romans 12:2,8;** *2 Do not be conformed to this world (this age), [fashioned after and adapted to its external, superficial customs], but be transformed (changed) by the [entire] renewal of your mind [by its new ideals and its new attitude], so that you may prove [for yourselves] what is the good and acceptable and perfect will of God, even the thing which is good and acceptable and perfect [in His sight for you]. 8 He who exhorts (encourages), to his exhortation; he who contributes, let him do it in simplicity and liberality; he who gives aid and superintends, with zeal and singleness of mind; he who does acts of mercy, with genuine cheerfulness and joyful eagerness.* **AMPC**

God does not want a broken will,

    a.  He wants a will wholly submitted to His will so that you can work in unity with Him.

    b.  How do we know Gods will for our life? The

Word.

    c. Your will gets in line with God's will by knowing what the Word says because the Word is His will.

4. The prosperity of your emotions takes place when you control them, not when they control you.

    a. This does not mean never showing any emotions.

    b. Jesus wept at Lazarus' tomb.

        1) He showed emotions but was not moved by them.

        2) He did not become grief stricken.

        3) He put his priorities where they belonged and raised Lazarus from the dead.

5. You will never be more prosperous than your mind. To live a prosperous life, your soul/mind must prosper in all truth of the Word.

6. There were several characters in the Bible who showed emotions. Jesus, Elijah, Elisah, David, and Joseph just to name a few.

## C. Physical Prosperity

1. This consists of health in your body.

2. God wants us to live in divine health because it is provided in the covenant and so that we can have the honor of giving of ourselves to Him as He has given of Himself to us. **Psalms 104:1-5**

    a. People who are sick tend to center on themselves rather than others.

    b.  Satan loves this, so he tries to cause us to be unhealthy.

    c.  It's hard to be effective when you are sick all the time and worrying about your health.

**NOTE**: You can have a truck load of soap delivered to your house and you can still stink like a skunk. The presence of soap does not make you smell good or change your appearance. The Word of God works the same way, it does not work in your life until it is applied!!

**D. The Word produces spiritual, mental, financial, and physical prosperity .**

1.  **Hebrews 4:12** tells us that the Word divides the soul and spirit and is a discerner of the thoughts and intents of the heart.

2.  **Joshua 1:8** *"This Book of the Law shall not depart from your mouth, but you shall meditate in it day and night, that you may observe according to all that is written in it.* <u>*For then you will make your way prosperous, and then you will have good success.*</u>*"*

3.  **Proverbs 4:20-22** *"My son, give attention to my words; Incline your ear to my sayings.* [21] *Do not let them depart from your eyes; Keep them in the midst of your heart;* [22] *For they are life to those who find them, And health to all their flesh."*

4.  **Psalms 107:20** *"He sent His word and healed them And delivered them from their destructions."*

5.  *As you grow in the light of the Word, you will become prosperous in your spirit, soul, and body.*

The Word of God must be absolute in your life. The only way to truly live a life of Biblical prosperity is to be a student of the Word. And if you are willing and obedient you shall eat the good of the land.

## Psalm 103:20

### Amplified Bible, Classic Edition

[20] Bless (affectionately, gratefully praise) the Lord, you His angels, you mighty ones who do His commandments, hearkening to the voice of His word.

Everything God created responded to his spoken Word!

Nothing was created, without words first being spoken.

# Chapter 2
# God's Will Is Prosperity

**Introduction:** "I have never met a lifetime tither who has regretted it and wanted a refund." (Mark Hankins) The life of prosperity began in the Garden of Eden. Man continues to be deceived by Satan. Our world is nowhere and nothing like what God had originally planned. God's plan was for man's life to be perfect in all ways. It was God's plan for man to never have lack. By Adam's own free will, he subjected and delivered himself and his kingdom that had been given to him, to Satan. We all fail at times because of our own free will.

## Genesis 3:17-19

I.  In the beginning (Genesis Chapters 1-3).

    A. **God placed everything that Adam could use and enjoy in the Garden of Eden**

        1. Adam lacked no good thing.

        2. God furnished him with companionship, ability, abundance, and a kingdom.

        3. He told Adam to be fruitful, multiply, fill the earth, subdue it, and have dominion over every living creature.

        4. He was free in every way and knew no bondage until he disobeyed God.

    B. **When he did this, he came under the bondage of Satan and corruption.**

        1. He was separated from God and lived under the

dominion of Satan whose nature is spiritual death.

2. By his own free will, he subjected himself and his kingdom to Satan.

By natural birth Adam's children, all humanity, would be born after his new nature of death and Satan (Romans 5:12,17). New King James Version

*12 Therefore, just as through one man sin entered the world, and death through sin, and thus death spread to all men, because all sinned —*

*17 For if by the one man's offense death reigned through the one, much more those who receive abundance of grace and of the gift of righteousness will reign in life through the One, Jesus Christ.)*

**C. Every phase of Adam's life came under the curse of his new father and god, satan.**

1. He was driven from the garden and abundance was no longer his to enjoy.

2. He had to toil and sweat to survive.

3. He now was subject to sickness, disease and lack. All three of these are a part of the curse talked about in Deut. 28. Our New Testament covenant removes that curse and all other curses listed in Deut. 28.

**D. God's will for Adam was abundance and plenty with no lack.**

1. The Lordship of God provided only good.

2. What is Lordship? Making Jesus first place in your life and then living a life pleasing to Him.

3. Poverty and lack came only after Adam changed gods and began to operate under Satan's dominion.

4. Satan is the author of poverty; God is the author of abundance. (You must choose Satan's poverty or God's abundance! It's literally your choice because of free will.

a. When Adam served God, all he knew was abundance; he had the best of everything.

b. **God's will for Adam was abundance.**

c. God's will does not change and His will for His people today is abundance (**James 1:17** *"Every good gift and every perfect gift is from above, and comes down from the Father of lights, with whom there is no variation or shadow of turning."*)

1. God's will has always been abundance for His people and He has continually provided freedom from the curse of poverty.

2. We put ourselves back under the curse by our disobedience and not believing God's Written Word. When His power is accessed through His Word.

3. Lordship in my opinion is the number one problem in people's lives. Until you totally submit your spirit, will and emotions to God, you are subject to live a life of lack and your needs not being met.

## II. The blessing of Abraham – Genesis 17:1-9

"When Abram was ninety-nine years old, the LORD appeared to Abram and said to him, "I am Almighty God; walk before Me and be blameless. 2 *And I will make My covenant between Me and you and will multiply you exceedingly."* 3 *Then Abram fell on his face, and God talked with him, saying:* 4 *"As for Me, behold, My covenant is with you, and you shall be a father of many nations. ⁵ No longer shall your name be called Abram, but your name shall be Abraham; for I have made you a father of many nations.* ⁶ *I **will make you exceedingly fruitful**; and I will make nations of you, and kings shall come from you.* ⁷ ***And I will establish My covenant between Me and you and your descendants after you in their generations, for an everlasting covenant, to be God to you and your descendants after you.*** ⁸ *Also I give to you and your descendants after you the land in which you are a stranger, all the land of Canaan, as an everlasting possession; and I will be their God."* ⁹ *And God said to Abraham: "As for you, **you shall keep My covenant, you and your descendants after you throughout their generations."***

1.  Vs. 7 "I will establish"

    a.  The definition for "establish" is to make steadfast, firm or stable; to settle on a firm or permanent basis; to set or fix unalterably.

    b.  God will make His covenant firm with the descendants of Abraham in this generation.

    c.  He will set or fix this covenant with you and me in our day to such a degree that the promise cannot be altered.

2.  Vs. 7 "To be God to you"

    a.  The blessing of God took care of Abraham physically and materially and had the promise of spiritual redemption.

    b.  The Bible says that Abraham was extremely rich.

        1)  ***Genesis 24:1*** *"Now Abraham was old, well advanced in age; and the LORD had blessed Abraham in all things."*

        2)  ***Proverbs 10:22*** *"The blessing of the LORD makes one*

> *rich, And He adds no sorrow with it."*

   c. Abraham had a covenant with God and walked upright before Him and nothing nor no one could successfully alter the promise of God because of the covenant.

**B. God said He would also establish His covenant with Abraham's descendants.**

   **1. Isaac**

      a. *Genesis 17:21 "…My covenant I will establish with Isaac…"*

      b. *Genesis 26:24 "And the LORD appeared to him the same night and said, "I am the God of your father Abraham; do not fear, for I am with you. I will bless you and multiply your descendants for My servant Abraham's sake."*

      c. *Genesis 26:13-14 "(Isaac) began to prosper, and continued prospering until he became very prosperous;* [14] *for he had possessions of flocks and possessions of herds and a great number of servants. So, the Philistines envied him."*

   **2. Jacob, Isaac's son.**

      a. *Genesis 30:43 "Thus (Jacob) became exceedingly prosperous, and had large flocks, female and male servants, and camels and donkeys."*

      b. Jacob's father-in-law cheated and deceived him for years, but that could not alter the covenant (**Genesis 31:7-12**).

   **3. Joseph, Jacob's son.**

      a. Joseph was sold into slavery by his brothers, but that

did not stop God from establishing His covenant with him (**Genesis 39:2-3** *"The LORD was with Joseph, and he was a successful man; and he was in the house of his master the Egyptian. 3 And his master saw that the LORD was with him and that the LORD made all he did to prosper in his hand."*)

   b.  Later the covenant prospered Joseph even in prison.

      1)  God gave him favor and the head of the prison put him in charge.

      2)  The Lord made whatever Joseph did to prosper (**Genesis 39:21-23**).

   c.  From prison, he was promoted to the office of governor, giving him full charge of the country (**Genesis 41:42-43**) *"Then Pharaoh took his signet ring off his hand and put it on Joseph's hand; and he clothed him in garments of fine linen and put a gold chain around his neck. 43 And he had him ride in the second chariot which he had; and they cried out before him, "Bow the knee!" So, he set him over all the land of Egypt."*).

4.  The Bible is clear about what the blessing of Abraham produced in the lives of Abraham, Isaac, Jacob, and Joseph.

   a.  The seed of Abraham was as blessed as Abraham.

   b.  These men were exceedingly wealthy.

   c.  They lived to be old and died satisfied (**Genesis 25:8, 35:29**).

**Amplified Bible, Classic Edition** *[8] Then Abraham's spirit was released, and he died at a good (ample, full) old age, an old **man, satisfied** and satiated, and was gathered to his people.*

*35:²⁹ And Isaac's spirit departed; he died and was gathered to his people, being an old man, satisfied and satiated with days; his sons Esau and Jacob buried him.*

5. God's dealings with Isaac, Jacob and Joseph were the results of the promise He made to establish the covenant with Abraham's descendants in their generation.

**C. The blessing of Abraham is also for this generation.**

1. The blessing of the covenant cannot be stopped in the life of an heir of Abraham (**Genesis 17:7** *"And I will establish My covenant between Me and you and your descendants after you in their generations"*).

2. God promised Abraham to establish His covenant with you and me in our generation.

   a. We are both descendants and heirs and God has obligated Himself to bless you as He blessed Abraham.

   b. Because of His promise, God will multiply you exceedingly and make you exceedingly fruitful.

   c. He has given His Word to prosper you the same way He prospered Abraham.

3. In order for God to fulfill what He promised Abraham, He must be allowed to prosper Abraham's descendants as though today were the day He made the promise (**Deuteronomy 8:18** *"18 "And you shall remember the LORD your God, for it is He who gives you power to get wealth, that He may establish His covenant which He swore to your fathers, as it is this day."*).

4. It is through Jesus that we receive the blessings (**Galatians 3:13-14, 26, 29** *"Christ has redeemed us from the curse of the*

*law, having become a curse for us (for it is written, "Cursed is everyone who hangs on a tree"), 14 that the blessing of Abraham might come upon the Gentiles in Christ Jesus, that we might receive the promise of the Spirit through faith. 26 For you are all sons of God through faith in Christ Jesus. 29* **And if you are Christ's, then you are Abraham's seed, and heirs according to the promise.")**

## III.  God's covenant is a covenant of prosperity.

A.  His covenant causes prosperity to be manifested in the earth (**Psalms 35:27** *"Let the LORD be magnified, who has pleasure in the prosperity of His servant."*)

B.  God cannot establish the covenant in your life unless you believe God's Word concerning prosperity (**Deuteronomy 29:9** *"Therefore keep the words of this covenant, and do them, that you may prosper in all that you do."*

C.  We have all the blessings of the Old Covenant and the power of the New.

1)  We have been born again with the nature of God.

2)  We are one spirit with the Lord.

3)  The Greater One lives in us.

4)  Jesus has recovered the authority Adam lost because of disobedience, and Satan has been defeated and put under our feet.

# Chapter 3
# The Laws of Prosperity – Part I

## The Laws of the Natural World and the Spiritual World

I.   The laws that govern the natural and spiritual worlds.

   A. **Natural world**

      1.   The laws of the natural world govern our activities.

         a)  We walk instead of floating.

         b)  If the law of gravity were not in action, we would float.

      2.   Natural physical laws can be manipulated.

<u>Example</u>:   The law of gravity is used when flying an airplane, but it is superseded by another law, the law of lift. When the law of lift is in operation, you can fly. But you must know something about the law of gravity to use the law of lift. You do not do away with the law of gravity; you just supersede it with a higher law.

**God's supernatural laws supersede all natural laws. (That's why we can confess and believe with confidence that God can and does make all things possible to those who believe.)**

   B. **Spiritual world.**

      1.   The spiritual world and its laws are more powerful than the natural world and its laws.

      2.   The natural world and its physical forces were created by the power of faith—a spiritual force

**(Hebrews 11:3** *"__By faith__ we understand that the worlds were framed by the word of God, so that the things which are seen were not made of things which are visible."*)

3. The law of gravity would be meaningless if gravity were not a real force.  In the same way, spiritual laws would be useless if the force of faith were not a real force.

4. Faith is a spiritual force, a spiritual energy, and a spiritual power.  It is the force of faith which makes the laws of the spirit world function.

5. **Romans 8:2** *"For the law of the Spirit of life in Christ Jesus has made me free from the law of sin and death." (It supersedes Death)*

   a) There are two functional laws in the spirit world — the law of sin and death and the law of the spirit of life.

      1) Adam put the first law into operation when he disobeyed God in the Garden of Eden

      2) Jesus put the second law into operation at His Resurrection

   b) The law of the spirit of life is the master law under which we operate as children of God. It supersedes the law of sin and death, and faith causes it to function.

   c) *Salvation is available to every human being (Joel 2:32, Amplified Bible, Classic Edition*

*32 And whoever shall call on the name of the Lord shall be delivered and saved, for in Mount Zion and in Jerusalem there shall be those who escape, as the Lord has said, and among the remnant [of survivors] shall be those whom the Lord calls.*

**Romans 10:13;** [13] *For everyone who calls upon the name of the Lord [invoking Him as Lord] will be saved.*

> 1) *This higher spiritual law of life (salvation) is here on earth, but every day people die and go to hell. Why?*

> 2) The law of salvation has not been put to work in their lives.

> 3) It will work <u>only</u> when it is put to work.

## II. The laws that govern prosperity.

A. The same rules that apply to all other spiritual laws apply to prosperity; they will work when they are put to work.

B. **1 Peter 1:25** *"The Word of the LORD endures forever"*; this is a law.

1. **When God speaks His words, they become law in the spiritual world.**

2. The success formulas in the Word of God produce results when used as directed.

3. **Mark 11:23** *"For assuredly, I say to you, whoever says to this mountain, `Be removed and be cast into the sea,' and does not doubt in his heart, but believes that those things he says will be done, he will have whatever he says."* **(Talking about spiritual laws)**

   a. Jesus introduced this principle — spiritual law — that works.

   b. It does not make sense to the natural mind that with faith you can have whatever you say. Even though it may be contrary to what you can see with your natural eye. Jesus said it and it is so.

   c.  When you act upon this principle of spiritual law. You speak the Word by mixing your faith with it. If you do not doubt in your heart, this spiritual law will work for you.

**For a law to work properly as designed, it must be applied and used properly or as designed.**

**The law of salvation does not work by our works, but by the law of faith. The law of faith must be applied for salvation to come to you and me.**

  **C.**  **The laws of prosperity work the same way as the laws of salvation, healing, etc.**

   1.  Any law God has ever revealed to His saints will never pass away.  **It will work every time it is put to work.**

   2.  Anything God taught Abraham or his descendants about operating financially will work just as well today as it did then.

  **D.**  Every law God has given us is recorded in His Word, and He has sent the Holy Spirit as our teacher to lead and guide us in these laws and show us how they operate so that we can put them to work.

  **E.**  Each time one of these laws operates, it glorifies God who spoke it and adds one more defeat to Satan who said it would not work.

  **F.**  Angels will also help us to operate by Gods Spiritual laws. I encourage you to read my book "Angels Are Among Us". It will help you understand how angels play a very important role in our daily lives.

# Chapter 4
# The Laws of Prosperity – Part 2

## The World's System vs. God's System

I.   Introduction

A. God has a highly organized system to meet the needs of every facet of your life.

    1. It works exactly opposite of the world's system.

    2. As believers we must be careful not to limit God in our lives to what the world says is so.

<u>Example</u>: Healing, when a doctor is honest, he will tell you that there is nothing he can do to heal a person; he can only treat the symptoms. There is no way to get healed except through the power of God. Either directly or by the power He built into the human body. No man can heal apart from God.

God designed many cells in our body to recreate or regenerate. Your heart will not regenerate itself, but it can heal itself. Medically speaking, not all human cells can regenerate in the natural. I do not doubt that God can replace them with healthy cells. But from a medical standpoint, some cells like the liver, can regenerate. Others, like neurons, skeletal muscle and cardiac cells are considered "permanent cells" because they are incapable of spontaneous regeneration.

Always take your medicine! God's Word is healing and a form of prosperity. God wants to prosper your health. To keep you healthy.

B. We have not known much about the law of the spirit of life. Not understanding it has caused problems in making it function for our benefit.

**C. To be successful at God's business, you must understand how His system works.**

   *1.* **Romans 12:2** *"And do not be conformed to this world, but be transformed by the renewing of your mind, that you may prove what is that good and acceptable and perfect will of God."*

   2. God's best will not come from the world's system. He will work around and through it to reach you, but it is always far below His best.

D. To properly study prosperity, you should never think of it from a worldly view.

   1. You must train yourself to think of it in line with God's Word.

   2. If you are not careful, when you think of the laws of prosperity, all you will see is money. This is only an exceedingly small part of prosperity.

**Let's take a minute and remember the definition of prosperity that we talked about in an earlier chapter, prosperity is having options, choices, to advance forward and to help succeed. It consists of spiritual, mental and physical prosperity. True prosperity is the ability to use God's Word, His Power to meet the needs of humanity in every realm of life.**

## II.  The world's system

A. To the world, prosperity, like everything else, is born of the senses or sense-ruled mind.

   1. The world is governed by natural impulse and the physical senses. Its slogan is "**seeing is believing**".

   2. If you can see it, taste it, smell it, or feel it, it must

be true; if you cannot contact it with your physical senses, it is not true.

B. The world's definition of prosperity is extremely limited in range, financial, political, social ability and power.

C. The World system does not have the power to overcome poverty, sickness, spiritual ills, or social ills.

D. In the world system, finances and prosperity can only come by your job, an inheritance, or other natural means. There is no supernatural involved.

E. It is up to you and me to break that mindset and change our way of not just thinking and doing, but also speaking.

## III. God's System.

To operate in God's financial system we will have to break the poverty mindset that we have been taught from birth. The first thing we hear and learn is NO, You can't, it's too expensive, we do not have the money. We are told from birth that we should just settle for whatever life brings us. We have to change that mindset to one of prosperity. God is our source, He created you and me to increase, dominate and multiply in this life.

A. As believers, we need to learn how to operate in God's system.

B. The power in God's system is prayer and the Word.

1. God's power is the only power that covers the entire spectrum of human existence.

2. You can pray in the Name of Jesus, and God will use His ability to handle your situation, whatever it is.

3. It takes the power of God to make you completely whole.

4. God used His Word to release His power. He has sent His Word so that we may be in contact with His great power (**Isaiah 55:11** *"So shall My word be that goes forth from My mouth; It shall not return to Me void, but it shall accomplish what I please, and it shall prosper in the thing for which I sent it."*)

5. Because God's power covers the entire range of human existence, so does His Word (**Hebrews 1:3** *"…upholding all things by the word of His power."*)

6. **Hebrews 4:12** reveals that the Word is a living thing which covers spirit, soul, body and our thought life. (All living things were designed to reproduce after themselves!)

7. **We must give voice to His Word. In other words, we must take action by faith to speak words. Not just any words but God's specific Words that bring healing, power, and prosperity.**

**C. A key principle in God's system is others before self.**

1. There is a basic, fundamental truth that runs throughout the Bible and throughout God's history of dealing with man.

   a) **Every time there was a need, no matter what the need was. God had a man somewhere who had the resources—spiritually, mentally, or financially—to meet that need.**

   b) For Israel there was Moses. For the world, there was Jesus. For Jesus there was a man with a donkey. For Ephesus, there was Paul.

2. **No one person will ever be so spiritual that he does not need other people. You can't do it by yourself!**

   a) **The key is to get your mind off self and your needs. Think about others and their needs. Luke 6:38** *"Give, and it will be given to you: good measure, pressed down, shaken together, and running over will be put into your bosom. For with the same measure that you use, it will be measured back to you."*

   b) When you begin to consider the needs of others before your own, your needs will be met supernaturally!

3. This principal deals with taking what you have and helping others.

a) If you know how to use God's ability to receive healing, help someone else get healed.

b) If you know how to believe God financially, start helping people around you.

c) Your faith in these and other areas will grow as you reach out to others.

**VIP. There is a reason I teach Faith, Healing, Prayer, Believers Authority, Doctrine of Angels and Prosperity is because it has worked for me. I can teach the principles that have worked for me and are taught in the Bible. But you must catch the spirit of each one of these for anything to change in your life.**

   D. **In John 14:18-23, Jesus gives the perfect outline of prosperity.**

   1. When God manifests Himself to you and lives with you, you are living in prosperity.

2. When we operate in the Word of God and keep His Word, Jesus will make Himself real to us.

3. He will not just be there; He will live in you. There is a difference.

4. If we put the Word first in our lives, whenever a problem arises in the physical realm, we will know the answer is in the Word and that the One living in us will put us over no matter how impossible the situation.

## NOTHING IS IMPOSSIBLE WITH GOD!

E. **Philippians 4:19** *says that God will meet our needs according to His riches in glory by Christ Jesus, not according to our need or our riches.*

1. Some preach that if you ask God for $100 but need only $20, He will just give you what you need and not what you are actually believing for. They don't believe we have a say in what we can have. They believe it has been predestined and we have no say about these things in our lives.

2. The Bible does not say that.

   a) **Isaiah 58:14 "...delight yourself in the LORD;** *And I will cause you to ride on the high hills of the earth,"*

   b) **Isaiah 1:19 "If you are willing and obedient,** *you shall eat the good of the land".*

   c) **Mark 11:24 "...whatever things you ask when you pray,** *believe that you receive them, and you will have them."*

> d) **James 4:2 "…you do not have because you do not ask.** [3] *You ask and do not receive, because you ask amiss."*
>
> e) **Psalms 37:4 "Delight yourself also in the LORD,** *And He shall give you the desires of your heart."*

F. When you act on the Word of God, the desires of your heart will begin to line up with God. Then He can cause all grace to abound toward you **(2 Corinthians 9:8).**

G. God is not limited to your job or any other natural means of getting finances to you unless you limit Him by your thinking.

H. Anyone can operate in the laws of prosperity.

I. They are not subject to age (young or old), culture, nor country.

**Faith is a spiritual force not subject to age, culture or country but works by spiritual law (Romans 3:27) Amplified Bible, Classic Edition** [27] *Then what becomes of [our] pride and [our] boasting? It is excluded (banished, ruled out entirely). On what principle? [On the principle] of doing good deeds? No, but on the principle of faith.*

J. All people are created equal.

K. The law of faith must be working in your life for any of the other Spiritual Laws or forces to work for you.

### Note

**No one can put a curse on you as a believer,**

**But you can open the door to a curse by disobedience and/or sin.**

**When sin, disobedience or unforgiveness is present a curse can and will follow you.**

**You can bring a curse on yourself as a believer.**

# Chapter 5
# The Principles of Prosperity

## James 4:7 & Psalms 37:13

### Amplified Bible, Classic Edition

### James 4:7

*7 So be subject to God. Resist the devil [stand firm against him], and he will flee from you.*

### Psalms 37:13

*13 The Lord laughs at [the wicked], for He sees that their own day [of defeat] is coming.*

I.    <u>Principle 1</u>. **Paying what belongs to God.**

  A. **Malachi 3:8-12** *"Will a man rob God? Yet you have robbed Me! But you say, `In what way have we robbed You?'* **In tithes and offerings.** *9 You are cursed with a curse, for you have robbed Me, even this whole nation. 10 Bring* **all the tithes into the storehouse,** *that* **there may be food in My house,** *and try Me now in this," Says the LORD of hosts, "If I will not open for you the windows of heaven and pour out for you such blessing That there will not be room enough to receive it. 11 "And I will rebuke the devourer for your sakes, so that he will not destroy the fruit of your ground, Nor shall the vine fail to bear fruit for you in the field," Says the LORD of hosts; 12 "And all nations will call you blessed, For you will be a delightful land," Says the LORD of hosts."*

  B. **Tithe in the Hebrew language means tenth.**

    1. **Giving 10% of your income to God is not optional.**

**It is mandatory according to scripture for a born-again believer.**

2. **A person who does not tithe is robbing God and is operating under a curse because of it.**

   a) If you have no finances, you can tithe your time, your produce, your work or anything else you have.

   b) When money does come, take out the part that belongs to God **first. (Proverbs 3:9,10 Amplified Version** *"Honor the Lord with your capital and sufficiency [from righteous labors], and with **the first fruits of all your income...** so shall your storage places be filled with plenty, and your vats be overflowing with new wine"*)

   c) God gets the first fruits of everything.

3. The tithe belongs to the storehouse; The place where you are being fed spiritual food. This normally would mean the local church you are attending. If the local church you are attending is not where you are getting your spiritual feeding, pray and ask the Lord where your tithe should go. **Note:** <u>If the above scenario is true for you, you are probably at the wrong church! Ask God where He wants you planted. Go there and tithe your tithe in that storehouse.</u>

4. **It is God's plan that the local church be supported by those who attend it so that it can fulfill God's vision for that church. It is up to the pastor of that church to share the vison he has with his congregation.**

5. **It is also God's plan that the pastor be supported by the members of the local body. (1 Corinthians 9:14** *"Even so the Lord has commanded that those who preach the gospel should live from the gospel."***)**

6. In **Malachi 3:10-11** *We are shown the rewards of the tither*

   a. God will bless them more than they have room to contain.

   b. He will rebuke Satan from stealing from them.

7. In tithing you are laying a foundation for financial success and abundance.

   a. You are establishing deposits with God that can be used when you need them.

   b. When we tithe, Satan's power over your finances is stopped. This does not mean Satan will not try to destroy your finances and prosperity, But when he does try, God will rebuke him and have your back.

C. **Offerings are what are given above the tithe and are given as the Holy Spirit leads. They are given to the poor and other ministries outside of the local church. sometimes as special projects of the local church or wherever else the Holy Spirit leads.**

   1. **Proverbs 19:17** *"He who has pity on the poor lends to the LORD, And He will pay back what he has given."*

      a. When you give to the Lord, you can expect back what you gave.

      b. You are lending to the Lord, and He will repay

you.

   c.  It is important to understand when giving to the poor, you want to give them more than just meeting their need of the day. Be sure and introduce them to THE need supplier. When you give someone meat to eat, it meets their need for that meal. When you teach a person how to hunt, you are providing the way for him to meet the need of all his meals.

2. **Mark 10:29-30** *"So Jesus answered and said, "Assuredly, I say to you, there is no one who has left house or brothers or sisters or father or mother or wife or children or lands, for My sake and the gospel's, 30  "who shall not receive a hundredfold now in this time----houses and brothers and sisters and mothers and children and lands, with persecutions----and in the age to come, eternal life.*

   a.  This is an investment into spreading the Gospel around the world.

   b.  **Mark 16:15** *says to go into all the world and preach the gospel to every creature.*

     1.  Every Christian is obligated to do this.

     2.  If you cannot go yourself, you are to send someone in your place. In reality, the Word says, "You Go". We are commanded to go into all the world and preach the Gospel. Do not let someone else get your blessing. Just do it.

     3.  Missionaries are instruments of God to evangelize the world. They deserve our support

both in finances, and prayer.

3. A third area of support is to the ministries who are teaching the Word of God through a traveling ministry. They are usually not supported by the local church and need outside finances to do the work God has called them to do.

## D. Six reasons to give tithes and offerings.

1. They show your dependence on God for His blessings and protection – **Malachi 3:10-11**

2. Regular giving keeps the windows of God's heaven open over your life – **Deuteronomy 8:18** *"And you shall remember the LORD your God, for it is He who gives you power to get wealth, that He may establish His covenant which He swore to your fathers, as it is this day."*

3. Jesus confirmed we should tithe in **Luke 11:42. Easy-to-Read Version** [42] *"But it will be bad for you Pharisees! You give God a tenth of the food you get, even your mint, your rue, and every other little plant in your garden. But you forget to be fair to others and to love God. These are the things you should do. And you should also continue to do those other things.*

4. The tithe represents your acknowledgement of God's ownership of everything – **Leviticus 27:30. Amplified Bible, Classic Edition**

[30] *And all the tithe of the land, whether of the seed of the land or of the fruit of the tree, is the Lord's; it is holy to the Lord.*

5. God has established the giving of tithes and offerings as the provision for meeting your every need – Philippians 4:19 is in direct correlation with the

Philippian church giving tithes and offerings.

*[19] And my God will liberally supply fill to the full your every need according to His riches in glory in Christ Jesus.*

## Psalms 37:13 Amplified Bible, Classic Edition

*[13] The Lord laughs at [the wicked], for He sees that their own day [of defeat] is coming.*

> **6.** *You are storing up treasures in heaven like a bank account to draw from when needed –* **Matthew 6:21. Amplified Bible, Classic Edition**

[21] For where your treasure is, there will your heart be also.

**E. Ways you should give.**

   **1.** Into every offering taken.

   **2.** Generously – **Luke 6:38, 2 Corinthians 9:6.**

   **3.** Cheerfully – **2 Corinthians 9:7.**

   **4.** Without a self-serving attitude.

   **a.** You should not give expecting God to return your giving with prosperity to spend on your own lusts.

   **b.** You should give with the attitude to get more money to give more to help others and to help spread the Gospel.

**F. You can never outgive God. Investing regularly in His work brings a return of 30, 60 and 100-fold. I challenge you to be a tither and a generous giver.**

**II.** Principle 2. Giving yourself totally to him

A. **Matthew 6:19-33 Amplified Version** *"Do not gather and heap* *up and store for yourselves treasures on earth, where moth and rust and worm consume and destroy, and where thieves break through and steal;* 20 *But gather and heap up and store for yourselves treasures in heaven, where neither moth nor rust nor worm consume and destroy, and where thieves do not break through and steal,* 21 ***For where your treasure is, there will your heart be also.*** 22 *The eye is the lamp of the body. So, if your eye is sound, your entire body will be full of light;* 23 *But if your eye is unsound, your whole body will be full of darkness. If then the very light in you [your conscience] is darkened, how dense is that darkness!* 24 *No one can serve two masters; for either he will hate the one and love the other, or he will stand by and be devoted to the one and despise and be against the other.* ***You cannot serve God and mammon [that is, deceitful riches, money, possessions or what is trusted in].*** 25 *Therefore, I tell you, stop being perpetually uneasy (anxious and worried) about your life, what you shall eat or what you shall drink, and about your body, what you shall put on. Is not life greater [in quality] than food, and the body [far above and more excellent] than clothing?* 26 *Look at the birds of the air; they neither sow nor reap nor gather into barns, and yet your heavenly Father keeps feeding them. Are you not worth more than they?* 27 *And which of you, by worrying and being anxious can add one unit of measure [cubit] to his stature or to the span of his life?* 28 *And why should you be anxious about clothes? Consider the lilies of the field and learn thoroughly how they grow; they neither toil nor spin;* 29 *Yet I tell you, even Solomon in all his magnificence (excellence, dignity, and grace) was not arrayed like one of these.* 30 *But if God so clothes the grass of the field, which today is alive and green and tomorrow is tossed into the furnace, will He not much more surely clothe you, O you men with little faith?* 31 *Therefore do not worry and be anxious saying, what are we going to have to eat? or, what are we going to have to drink? or, what are we going to have to wear?* 32 *For the*

*Gentiles (heathen) wish for and crave and diligently seek after all these things; and your heavenly Father well knows that you need them all. [33] But seek for (aim at and strive after) first of all His kingdom, and His righteousness [His way of doing and being right], and then all these things taken together will be given you besides."*

1.  The subject of this passage is how to oversee material things such as treasures, riches, possessions, food, drink, and clothes.

2.  God is not against a man having money; He is against money having the man. You can overcome being greedy by being generous.

3.  He is not opposed to people being rich; He is opposed to people being covetous or greedy. (**Luke 12:15** *"And He said to them, "Take heed and beware of covetousness, for one's life does not consist in the abundance of the things he possesses."*)

4.  All good things come from above. God wants and expects you and me to enjoy His Blessings. **We are royalty.**

**B. Your affection is not to be in your prosperity, business, goods, treasures, or holdings.**

In **Luke 12:16-21**: Jesus tells a parable about a wealthy man who continued to lay up or hoard possessions for himself. He did not remember it was God who had given him the power to get wealth. The land he owned produced so much that all his storehouses were full. He did not have room to store anymore. He decided to tear down his storehouses and build bigger ones. Then He said, *"Now I have good things laid up for many years. I can live the way I want to."* But God said to him, *"Fool! This night your soul will be required of you; then who will have those things which* *you have provided? "So, it is with him who continues to lay up and hoard possessions for himself and is not rich [in his relationship] to God this is how he fares"* (Amplified Version).

**C. Remember at the beginning we defined true prosperity as "the ability to use the power of God to meet the needs of mankind".**

1. If a man needs healing, money will not help him.

2. If his body is well but he has no money to pay the rent, God's healing power will not cover his need.

3. **God's plan for us is to have <u>all</u> our needs met according to His riches in glory by Christ Jesus (Philippians 4:19).**

4. True prosperity is having every need met and having options in this life.

**D. For God's laws of prosperity to work in your life, you must be spiritually ready to prosper.**

1. Throughout the Bible, God's people prospered when they obeyed His Word, but when they were disobedient, His laws of prosperity did not work for them.

2. If things are not working for you according to the Bible, check yourself and see if you are in disobedience. Most of the people's problems that found themselves in the desert for 40 years was because of their complaining and disobedience to Gods commandment.

3. They were still His people, but His powerful blessing was not manifested in their lives.

4. You can be saved on your way to heaven and not prosper in your health or your wealth.

5. God's laws of prosperity will work in the life of any

person who is obedient to His Word.

**PRAY AND OBEY - PRAY AND OBEY - PRAY AND OBEY**

**E. You will not prosper by believing only the part of God's Word concerning material blessing. You must believe it all.**

F. God's prosperity will work only in the life of the believer who is committed to the Word because he loves God, not for material gain.

## III. <u>Principle 3</u>. We Must Be Pleasing God.

**A. In Matthew 6:21 we read that your heart is where your treasure is. Vs. 22 goes on to say the eye is the lamp of the body and if your eye is sound, your body is sound.**

1. In the context of the passage, this is talking about possessions and material goods.

2. **Proverbs 4:20-22 Amplified Version** *"My son, attend to my words; consent and submit to my sayings. Let them not depart from your sight; keep them in the center of your heart. For they are life to those who find them, healing, and health to all their flesh."*

3. **Proverbs 7:2** *"Keep my commandments, and life; and my law as the apple of your eye."*

   a. The apple or pupil is the center of your eye.

   b. The sound eye stays on the Word of God.

   c. This is how you keep sound when materially prosperous.

**B. You are to keep your eye on God's Word.**

1. **Matthew 6:24** explains why: You cannot serve two masters.

   a. You cannot serve God and mammon (deceitful riches, money, possessions).

   b. When you put your eye on, or give attention to riches and material possessions, you will begin to serve them instead of them serving you.

2. **Colossians 3:1-2** *"If then you were raised with Christ, seek those things which are above, where Christ is, sitting at the right hand of God. 2 Set your mind on things above, not on things on the earth."*

   a. In this passage, we are instructed to seek or set our affections on the things which are above.

   b. We are to set our affections to serve God, not riches.

   c. Money should not control your thinking or actions.

3. **Mark 4:18-19** *"Now these are the ones sown among thorns; they are the ones who hear the word, 19 and the cares of this world, the deceitfulness of riches, and the desires for other things entering in choke the word, and it becomes unfruitful."*

If your affection is set on wealth and riches instead of God, the Word becomes unfruitful in your life. Greed is a tool of Satan to choke the Word and make it powerless in your life. The Word cannot bear fruit in a person who has his affections set on the things of the earth.

   C. **When you set your affection on things that are above, your spiritual life will be intact, and all other things** will be yours to enjoy as well.  The possessions that are added to you will serve you instead of you serving them.

**D.** This is a person who is rich toward God.

## IV. <u>Principle 4.</u> We Must Seek God's Kingdom and His Righteousness

**A.** Matthew 6:25 tells us to stop being anxious and worried over things (food, clothes, material possessions).

1. You are to have an attitude of trust and faith concerning material things.

2. You are not to try to figure out how God is going to meet your needs.

3. You are not to seek after things like ungodly people do. Why?

   a. You have a covenant with God.

   b. God knows what you have need of and delights in providing for you (**Psalms 35:27** *"Let them shout for joy and be glad, who favor my righteous cause; And let them say continually, "Let the LORD be magnified, who has pleasure in the prosperity of His servant."*)

   **c. Psalm 37:3 Amplified Bible, Classic Edition**

*3 Trust (lean on, rely on, and be confident) in the Lord and do good; so shall you dwell in the land and feed surely on His faithfulness, and truly you shall be fed.*

**B.** Matthew 6:33 tells us to seek first the kingdom of

**God and His righteousness.**

1. You do this by committing to obey whatever you see in His Word.  The Word is full of integrity. You can depend on the word of a doctor, lawyer, or best friend.

2. If you are going to commit to do what the Word says, you must commit to every part of it. You must become a student of the Word. Know it for yourself, from start to finish.

   a. The Word of God will produce just as far as you dare to commit to it.

   b. It will make you free when you commit to it.

   c. There is power, peace, provision, and prosperity in God's word.

# V. Refresh yourself with this summary of what we have already covered.

## A. Summary of the steps to pleasing God and putting Him first.

1. Keep your eyes focused  on the Word of God.

2. Do not allow possessions or lack of them to get your attention.

3. Do not try to serve two masters: God and mammon.

4. Do not trust in money but the Word of God.

5. Do not be worried or anxious about anything.

6. Seek first the kingdom of God and His righteousness.

## B. Do not follow these steps to become prosperous but to

**operate scripturally by the Word of God.**

1. You cannot simply decide to take the promise of prosperity from God's Word and live by that, ignoring the part about living a dedicated life before God.

2. Prosperity will not work for you if you are not seeking first the kingdom of God.

**C. 3 John 2** *"Beloved, I pray that you may prosper in all things and be in health, just as your soul prospers."*

1. **You will prosper only to the degree your soul prospers.**

2. Bible prosperity will not come any other way.

3. The laws of prosperity are based on obedience to God's Word. **BONUS NOTES**

**We have been given a responsibility to help the poor.**

1. The New Testament Christian has a responsibility to the poor and disadvantaged. <u>How will you be able to accomplish this without money and/or prosperity?</u>

2. God instructs all His people in the New Testament to Love and show a deep concern, to show compassion for those in need. Especially those within the church community of believers.

3. Much of Jesus ministry was to the poor and disadvantaged people of His time. The people no one else cared about.

**Luke 4:18-19**; The used, misused and oppressed.

**Luke 17:11-19**; The Samaritans

**Matthew 8:2-4**; The people with leprosy

**Luke 7:11-15**; The widows

There were many others who were disadvantaged, materially, financially, and socially that Jesus helped. Jesus had harsh words for those who took advantage of the poor and the people in these situations we have just talked about. Jesus expected His followers to give generously to those in need.

**Matthew 6:1-4**; On more than one occasion he instructed His disciples and  followers to give to the needy. He kept a money bag for this purpose. The early church on many occasions showed active compassion to those in need, During Paul's 3rd missionary journey one of his goals was to gather or raise money for the poor saints in Jerusalem.

1. Our priority in caring for the poor is to meet the needs of follow Christians who need help before we help the worldly people.

2. The Bible gives us no choice but to be sensitive to the material needs of those people around us.

3. Many people who are not open to knowing Christ will not be open until someone who does know Him takes the time to meet their need.

**PEOPLE DON'T CARE HOW MUCH YOU KNOW UNTIL YOU SHOW HOW MUCH YOU CARE!**

# Chapter 6
# Divine Prosperity

**I. God works in our behalf.**

A. **2 Corinthians 9:8 Amplified Version** *"And God is able to make all grace (every favor and earthly blessing) come to you in abundance, so that you may always and under all circumstances and whatever the need, be self-sufficient possessing enough to require no aid or support and furnished in abundance for every good work and charitable donations"*

1. The Word says God is able to get all finances to you. **Do not look to natural resources or your job.**

2. You must keep your eye totally on the Word only.

3. You must realize and know that He can and will work on your behalf.

4. The world's system may seem to be the easier way. In the long run God's way is not only easier but far more superior.

5. Why not start with asking God what He wants us to do. How to do it and when to do it. God's plan is always perfect, peaceful and prosperous.

B. **When you need something and ask, God starts to work immediately.**

**We know God hears our prayers, and the Word says He will answer.**

1. There may be no evidence of it for you to see, but you must look to the Word for evidence and not

circumstances.

2. When you pray God's Word it activates Angels, the Holy Spirit and all His promises. Things begin to work in your behalf. God's Word works every-time.

3. When you believe God for something, do not waver. Expect to receive. Faith is now! Began to speak the Word over that situation and take action as God will reveal a plan of action to you.

4. Make a quality decision the Word is true. This is crucial to your success.

5. How long will you have to stand on God's Word to get your needs met?

6. Kenneth Hagin once said, "If you are determined to stand forever, it will not take long."

**C. When you take the step of faith to believe God and His Word, He will make sure you have the revelation knowledge of His Word to make it come about.**

Knowledge is great but Revelation Knowledge activates the Supernatural! We get natural knowledge from natural sources (sight, smell, touch and emotions just to name a few). Revelation knowledge can only come from God The Father, God the Son and/or The Holy Spirit.

**Note:** If a Holy Angel brings you wisdom and knowledge it will always line up with God's Word. It will line up with what He brings through His Word or Revelation that He brings to you. But it will never contradict the written Word of God.

**D. A key in getting your needs met is to make the commitment to stay out of debt and never waver on that commitment (Romans 13:8** *"Owe no one anything* *except to love one another," – another version says, "keep out of debt and owe no man anything".*

## II.Redeemed from the curse. Confess daily you are redeemed from the curse of the law.

A. **Poverty and lack are a part of the curse of the law. Deuteronomy describes the curse of the law in Deuteronomy 28.**

1. **Deuteronomy 28:29-30, 33, 44, 15 Amplified Version**
   *[15] All these curses shall come upon you and shall pursue you and overtake you "[29] And you shall grope at noonday, as the blind grope in darkness, and you shall not prosper in your ways; and you shall be only oppressed and robbed continually, and there shall be no one to save you [30] you shall build a house, and not live in it. [33] A nation which you have not known shall eat up the fruit of your land and of all your labors; and you shall be only oppressed and crushed continually…[44] He (the stranger) shall lend to you, and you shall not lend to him; he shall be the head, and you shall be the tail. ."*

B. **We have been redeemed from the curse of the law through Jesus – Galatians 3:13-14** *"Christ has redeemed us from the curse of the law, having become a curse for us (for it is written, "Cursed is everyone who hangs on a tree"),14 that the blessing of Abraham might come upon the Gentiles in Christ Jesus,"*

C. **The blessing of Abraham included a financial blessing; the curse of the law included financial reversal.** You must decide what you believe. The Word will react according to your beliefs and confessions of that Word.

**III. A revelation of divine prosperity.**

    **A. When you think of divine prosperity, you must look at it in the same way you look at every other blessing from God.**

        1. When you are walking in divine health and a symptom of sickness comes to your body, you can take authority over it immediately and do not allow it to stay. By doing so, you walk in divine health.

        2. You must do the same thing when it comes to your finances and your spiritual well-being.

    **B. Divine prosperity works the same way.**

        1. You cannot allow symptoms of lack to come upon you and stay

        2. If you fail to act accordingly to the Word, you fail by default.

        3. Jesus bore the curse of poverty at the same time He bore the curse of sickness. <u>Both blessings belong to you</u>.

        4. You should refuse lack just as quickly as you refuse sickness.

        5. Since Jesus bore the curse of poverty, we should always have enough. He provided prosperity for us. Whatever Jesus took or bore on the cross for you, you don't have to bear that burden anymore. He relieved you and me of the burden of sickness, sin, pain and poverty. He will keep it unless you take it back. If you want to bear those burdens you can always take them back by not believing His

Word or improper confessions. Remember: We are hung by our tongue. We can speak blessing or we can speak cursing. Whatever we speak, we shall have. We shall reap what we sow or speak..

**C. Isaiah 1:19 *"If you are willing and obedient, you shall eat the good of the land"***

1.  The word "willing" is an action word. It involves a decision.

2.  If you are willing, you have determined to live that way.

3.  You can be willing but not obedient! You can also be obedient but not willing. Scripture tells us when we are willing and obedient we will eat the good of the land.

4.  Once you make a quality decision that you are not willing to live in lack. You can operate in divine prosperity and abundance. Satan cannot stop the flow of God's financial blessings. Satan is not all powerful. Actually the Bible says he is a defeated foe.

    a.  You can make that decision because the Word provides prosperity and abundance for you.

    b.  You are an heir of the blessing of Abraham.

    c.  Redemption from the curse of poverty is part of Jesus' substitutionary work at Calvary.

    d.  **He willingly paid the price for your prosperity.**

5.  You begin to walk in divine prosperity with a

decision to allow satan no longer to put symptoms of lack on you.

## IV. Peace and prosperity.

A. **Isaiah 53:5 Amplified Version** *"But He was wounded for our transgressions, He was bruised for our guilt and iniquities; the chastisement needful to obtain peace and well-being for us was upon Him, and with the stripes that wounded Him we are healed and made whole."*

    1. Jesus bore the chastisement needed to obtain peace and well-being.

    2. **Peace and well-being include whatever you need, including prosperity**.

    3. You cannot enjoy peace and well-being if you do not have your needs met.

B. **Isaiah 48:18 Amplified Version** *"Oh, that you had hearkened to My commandments! Then your peace and prosperity would have been like a flowing river."*

    1. Peace and well-being include a prosperous life.

    2. In **Genesis 15:1 Amplified Version** God told Abram *"Fear not, Abram, I am your shield, **your abundant compensation**, and your reward shall be exceedingly great"*.

## Definitions:

**Fear not**: It means we are not to allow anxiety or fretfulness to rule our lives or take root in it.

**Shield:** A person or thing providing protection.

**Abundant**: Existing or available in large quantities; plentiful.

**Compensation**: Something, typically money, awarded to someone as a recompense for loss, injury, or suffering.

**Reward**: A thing given in recognition of one's service, effort, or achievement.

**Shall**: Expressing an instruction or command.

**Exceedingly:** To a great extent.

**Great:** Of an extent, amount, or intensity considerably above the normal or average.

In other words God told Abraham. I will protect you and not only protect you but I will bring to you quantities of money and other rewards. This is a command and it will be to a great extent, above the average or normal.

This should excite you and me. We are heirs to Abraham and everything God promised Abraham is also promised to you and me.

> **3. Abundant compensation is far reaching and means everything.**

> **C. Peace and prosperity go hand in hand.**

>> 1. Prosperity is yours!

>> 2. It is not something you have to strive to work toward.

>> 3. When He paid the price of sin, He also paid the price for the curse of poverty so that you can be free from sin and prosperous/rich.

## V. How to walk in divine prosperity.

> **A. Treat any symptom of lack just as you would treat a symptom of sickness.**

>> 1. The very moment a symptom shows up in your life, take authority over it. (Financially, Health, Mentally

and Spiritually)

2. Command it to flee from you in the Name of Jesus, then stand your ground.

3. **Submit to God**, resist the devil and he will have to flee as in terror **James 4:7**.

**This scripture is misquoted by many Christians, and they don't even realize it. The Bible says:**

*7 So be subject to God. Resist the devil [stand firm against him], and he will flee from you* Most people including Christians leave off the submit or be subject to God part. You cannot resist the devil in the natural world, in your own wisdom and strength. He will not obey you or your words. He will obey when we submit to God first, and then resist him with God's Words. **Amplified Bible, Classic Edition**

## Memorize this.

Say: Father, I submit my life to you, to Jesus and the Holy Spirit. "Lack, I resist you in the Name of Jesus. I command you to flee from me. I have been redeemed from the curse of poverty and lack. I will not tolerate you in my life!"

**B. We Must Take dominion.**

*1.* You have the same authority over the earth that Adam had in the Garden of Eden. **Genesis 1:27-28 Amplified Version** *"So God created man in His own image, <u>in the image and likeness of God He created him;</u> male and female He created them. And God blessed them, and said to them, be fruitful, multiply, and fill the earth and subdue it [with all its vast resources; **and have dominion over the fish of the sea, the birds of the air, and over every living creature that moves upon the earth."**

2.  God made the earth and then man. Then He gave man dominion and authority over it. It is man's earth (**Psalms 115:16** *"The heaven, even the heavens, are the LORD'S; But the earth He has given to the children of men."*)

3.  God said subdue it and have dominion over its vast resources.

4.  Anything you can see with your eyes comes from the earth's resources. **You cannot have a material need that the earth's resources cannot handle.**

5.  Jesus came to give us back our earthly authority. It is up to you and me to take and use that authority. Satan is the God of this world, but we have been given authority and power over him and his followers.

C.  **"There is no way is a common statement." With God there is always a way of escape. Always!**

A.  **This statement should not be in your vocabulary.**

1.  When you think there is no way, it is coming from Satan, not God.

2.  God will never tell you there is no way. Jesus said, **_"I am the way."_** (**John 14:6**)

B.  **The Word of God is the source of our prosperity.**

Do not look to people to meet your needs; look to the Word. Satan will try to convince you that you can never walk in prosperity. Do not look at the circumstances around you. Look at the Word that says it is yours. Stop saying: I cannot afford that. Instead say: What do I need to do differently to be able to afford or get what I need or want. God not only wants to supply your needs. He wants to supply your wants and desires.

**C. Do not just believe God to meet your needs. Believe in Him for a surplus of prosperity so that you can help others.**

If you are furnished in abundance, then you will be able to reach out to others. You will live in a surplus of prosperity and walk in divine prosperity.

## YOU ARE BLESSED

That is why money is so important to minister's and missionaries. It takes money to take the Gospel around the world. It takes money to have the resources to help the poor and needy. In other words, it takes money to do whatever it is God has given you and I to do. Money is not  bad; it is a tool for us to use to our benefit.

# Chapter 7
# Walking in Prosperity

## I.Introduction:

A.  To walk in prosperity in all areas of your life, you must believe God.

You must know His Word and How to use it to your advantage.

You were not created to live a life of average or mediocrity. You were created and destined for greatness and abundance.

Stop listening to the nay sayers, your mommy, brother, pastor, or bishop who is speaking negatively. Speaking doubt and telling you to just accept your lot in life is a lie from the devil himself. The God we serve is a God of more, a God of abundance. He expects you and me to operate in that abundance.

## Just stop it.

Get as far away from these people as you can. They have already succumbed to a lifestyle and mindset of lack and defeat.

You were destined, designed, and deployed for increase, to dominate and multiply here in this life..

Go to Genesis 1:26-28 and look at the very first Word or command that God gave man after he was created. Amplified Bible *26 Then God said, "Let Us (Father, Son, Holy Spirit) make man in Our image, according to Our likeness [not physical, but a spiritual personality and moral likeness]; and let them have complete authority over the fish of the sea, the birds of the air, the cattle, and over the entire earth, and over everything that creeps and crawls on the earth." 27 So God created man in His own image, in the image and likeness of God He created him; male and female He created them. 28 And God blessed them [granting them certain* *authority] and said to them, "Be fruitful, multiply, and fill the earth, and subjugate it [**putting it under your power]; and rule over (dominate)** the fish of the sea, the birds of the air, and every living thing that moves upon the earth."*

We find clear instructions here: Be fruitful and produce, multiply (this means in every area of your life), fill the earth, put it under our power and rule and reign and dominate over it. God gave us charge over everything He made and put it under our authority.

Inside each of you beats the heart of the Lion of Judah (if you are Born Again!)

# VIP:   MONEY operates in the spiritual realm, it is a spiritual battle for a Christians.

The reason many Christians struggle financially, they have only been attacking it from a natural standpoint, When we fight the wrong battle the wrong way we get wrong results. There are over one hundred scriptures in the Bible that tells us to bless the poor in one way or another. How can we help the poor if we are among the poor? If you are always broke you will not help the poor. If God really wanted us to be poor, he would not have asked or expected us to help the poor. No, he expects us to operate in the spirit realm financially and be blessed.

Some people think it is a sin to have money, wealth, or riches! In Deut. 8:18 it says;

(Amplified *Bible*) [18] *But you shall [earnestly]* <u>remember the Lord your God, for it is He Who gives you power to get wealth,</u> *that He may establish His covenant which He swore to your fathers, as it is this day. .*

**Corinthians 8:9 Amplified Version says:** [9] *For you are recognizing [more clearly] the grace of our Lord Jesus Christ [His astonishing kindness, His generosity, His gracious favor<u>, that though He was rich, yet for your sake He became poor, so that by His poverty you might become rich (abundantly blessed).</u>*

Jesus personally took away our poverty so that we could be made rich. Why would he do that if being rich was sin? Why did He command the financial blessing on us in <u>Deut. 28:8-11</u>?

**God hated poverty so much he made it a part of the curse in Deut. 28. Then Jesus took poverty upon Himself on the cross so that we might be made rich here in this life.**

**Most people including Christians misquote 1 Timothy 6:10 and believe that money is the root of all evil, that money itself is evil. That is not what that scripture says or means.** (Amplified Bible [10] *For the love of money [that is, the greedy desire for it and the willingness to gain it unethically] is a root of all sorts of evil, and some by longing for it have wandered away from the faith and pierced themselves [through and through] with many sorrows*).

**Money is not the root of evil; the love of money is a root of evil.**

**If you have a great hunger for God and all His laws, commandments and statues you will not have a love of money.**

**John 10:10** is another scripture that proves Jesus came so that you might have joy and abundance, to the full, until it overflows. Amplified Bible

[10] *The thief comes only to steal and kill and destroy. I came that they may have and enjoy life, and have it in abundance [to the full, till it overflows].*

**It's time you commit to going all in and believing the Word. Speak the Word and act as if the Word is true. It must be the first place in your heart and life.**

**GOD WANTS YOU TO HAVE INCREASE IN YOUR LIFE!**

1. The predominant rule about believing God is **Romans 10:17** *"Faith comes by hearing, and hearing by*

*the word of God."*

2. Acting on God's Word brings results, not sometimes, but EVERY TIME.

3. You should act on His Word as quickly as you would the word of a doctor, lawyer, or trusted friend. Regardless of circumstances or what your physical senses say, believe the Word of God over all circumstances..

4. In other words, take your medicine and DO WHAT THE Word says to do.

5. What did Jesus' Mother tell the servants at the wedding when they asked her what to do about them running out of wine? She said, find Jesus and then ask Him what to do. When he tells you, follow His instruction and do exactly as he says to do. We all know what happened when they followed Jesus' instruction. It happened just as he said it would. This will work in our lives also. Just follow the direction or instruction of the Word and it will work.

B. **Acting upon God's Word as The Truth brings forth faith. When faith comes into action, it causes the laws of the Spirit World to function and bring results.** Sometimes taking action in the Spiritual Realm will cause the Spiritual Law to supersede the natural laws trying to dominate our lives.

C. **All Spiritual Laws will work for everyone, every time they are applied according to the Word.**

## II. Mark chapter 4 includes "the parable of the Sower (Mark 4:14-20)".

A. This chapter is about the Word of God and how the Word brings fruit.

B. **Vs. 15** - *And these are the ones by the wayside where the word is sown. When they hear, Satan comes immediately and takes away the word that was sown in their hearts.*

   1. The seed, the Word of God, does its job. It goes into our hearts and it always produces a harvest.

   2. **That is why satan comes quickly to take it away. He fears the Word.**

   3. Satan will *immediately* come to take away the Word sown.

C. **Vs. 16-17** - *These likewise are the ones sown on stony ground who, when they hear the word, immediately receive it with gladness and they have no root in themselves, and so endure only for a time. Afterward, when tribulation or persecution arises for the word's sake, immediately they stumble.*

   1. This is believers who have no confidence in themselves as believers.

   2. They endure for a little while but when persecution or tribulation comes, they stumble.

   3. When you begin operating according to the Word, Satan will do everything he can to defeat you. **The Word will fight its own fight** and cause you to be more than a conqueror. **(Romans 8:37) Amplified Bible, Classic Edition** [37] *Yet amid all these things we are more than conquerors [a]and gain a surpassing victory*

*through Him Who loved us.*

We do not have to fight our own battles. The Bible says we are to fight the good fight of faith. When we do, the Word will go to battle for us and the Word will always win.

> **4. The Word was spoken, so it could be written, so it could be spoken.**

> **(Never Forget this)**

5. The only thing we are required to do is speak God's Word. Then believe and expect it to work as God designed it to.

D. **Mark 4: 18-19** *"Now these are the ones sown among thorns; they are the ones who hear the word, and the cares of this world, the deceitfulness of riches, and the desires for other things entering in to choke the word, and it becomes unfruitful.*

Of the three categories listed in this passage, **the cares of the world are the most dangerous and capable to totally defeat you in your Christian walk.** Do not be deceived; be careful what you do. Where you do it, how you do it and who you do it with. These things can stop your faith. They will stop the Word in your life. You're stinking thinking will cripple your insides.

**The worldliest care is** *strife.* Strife is the lack of love and is the number one tool of Satan. We must walk in love. **Hatred, bitterness and unforgiveness will stop all God's blessing, materially and spiritually.**

**Mark 11:25-26; Amplified Bible, Classic Edition**

²⁵ *And whenever you stand praying, if you have anything against anyone, forgive him and let it drop (leave it, let it go), in order that your Father Who is in heaven may also forgive you your [own]*

*failings and shortcomings and let them drop.*

> a. **James 3:16:** For where envy and self-seeking exist, confusion and every evil thing are there.

> b. **Galatians 5:19-21** lists it among the lusts of the flesh.

**Amplified Bible, Classic Edition**

[19] *Now the doings (practices) of the flesh are clear (obvious): they are immorality, impurity, indecency,* [20] *Idolatry, sorcery, enmity, strife, jealousy, anger (ill temper), selfishness, divisions (dissensions), party spirit (factions, sects with peculiar opinions, heresies),* [21] *Envy, drunkenness, carousing, and the like. I warn you beforehand, just as I did previously, that those who do such things shall not inherit the kingdom of God.*

> a. **Mark 11:25-26** *"And whenever you stand praying, if you have anything against anyone, forgive him, that your Father in heaven may also forgive you your trespasses.* [26] *"But if you do not forgive, neither will your Father in heaven forgive your trespasses."*

> b. **Unforgiveness and strife are under the law of sin and death.**
>
>> 1) Each time a person operates in strife or unforgiveness, they submit to this law.
>>
>> 2) You cannot get God's forgiveness until you forgive and get the strife out of your life.
>>
>> 3) Satan knows how this works and will try to keep you in strife and unforgiveness.

**VIP.** This is crucial to your spiritual, physical, and financial wellbeing. It can keep you from living a prosperous and successful life.

a) Make up your mind now you will never operate in any area of unforgiveness.

**1. Faith works by love.**

The instant you get into strife will be the very instant your faith will begin to falter. It does not matter what people have done to you, love them in spite of it.

a. Give love and you will get love.

b. It may take a while, but it will come because love never fails.

E. **Mark 4:20** *"But these are the ones sown on good ground, those who hear the word, accept it, and bear fruit: some thirtyfold, some sixty, and some a hundred."*

F. **Vs. 21** *"…Is a lamp brought to be put under a basket or under a bed? Is it not to be set on a lampstand?" The lamp represents God's Word, we know this because the parable about the sower right above this scripture is about the Word.*

G. **Vs. 23-25** *""If anyone has ears to hear, let him hear." 24 Then He said to them, "Take heed what you hear. With the same measure you use, it will be measured to you; and to you who hear, more will be given. 25 "For whoever has, to him more will be given; but whoever does not have, even what he has will be taken away from him."*

H. **You will be held accountable for what you know and do not do!!! It is our responsibility to know God's Word. We must know His commandments, His statutes and His plan for mankind. We will not be able to stand before the Lord on judgement day and say, I did not know! He has given us a book full of wisdom and instructions. We must make a decision to read it and ask for wisdom and understanding.**

1. His Word has been provided so that we can live a life of abundance..

2. God has provided everything necessary to make you a success in this world as well as the one to come. All wisdom and knowledge comes to us through His Word and it has been made available to you and me. Now it is our responsibility to know, learn and do.

3. The Word provides the knowledge needed to govern Satan who is the thief who comes to kill, steal, and destroy (**John 10:10**).

4. **When we are sick, we do not need more doctors; we need more of the Word. When we have financial problems, we do not need more bankers; we need more of the Word. God's Word is the answer to every problem and situation we may face in this life.**

5. It is important you, as a believer, understand your covenant with God. The Word says healing and prosperity have been provided for you through Jesus. If you do not believe this, Satan will take what little you do have.

I. **Mark 4:26-29** *"And He said, "The kingdom of God is as if a man should scatter seed on the ground, 27 "and should sleep by night and rise by day, and the seed should sprout and grow, he himself does not know how. 28 "For the earth yields crops by itself: first the blade, then the head, after that the full grain in the head. 29 "But when the grain ripens, immediately he puts in the sickle, because the harvest has come."*

1. Do not block God's grace by saying "I cannot ask God to give me anything." You need to allow God to

bless you.

2. **The Bible says we have not because we ask not and we ask amiss. Always ask with the right motive. Approach God with humility and a correct motive.**

3. You plant the seed and then harvest the crop, **in God's timing. It's a spiritual law!**

J. **Vs. 30-33** *"To what shall we liken the kingdom of God? Or with what parable shall we picture it? 31 "It is like a mustard seed which, when it is sown on the ground, is smaller than all the seeds on earth; 32 "but when it is sown, it grows up and becomes greater than all herbs, and shoots out large branches, so that the birds of the air may nest under its shade." 33 And with many such parables He spoke the word to them as they were able to hear it."*

## III. Luke 6:27-38        VIP

A. *"I say to you who hear: Love your enemies, do good to those who hate you, 28 "bless those who curse you, and pray for those who spitefully use you. 29 "To him who strikes you on the one cheek, offer the other also. And from him who takes away your cloak, do not withhold your tunic either. 30 "Give to everyone who asks of you. And from him who takes away your goods do not ask them back. 31 "And just as you want men to do to you, you also do to them likewise. 32 "But if you love those who love you, what credit is that to you? For even sinners love those who love them. 33 "And if you do good to those who do good to you, what credit is that to you? For even sinners do the same. 34 "And if you lend to those from whom you hope to receive back, what credit is that to you? For even sinners lend to sinners to receive as much back. 35 But love your enemies, do good, and lend, hoping for nothing in return; and your reward* *will be great, and you will be sons of the Most High. For He is kind to the unthankful and evil. 36 "Therefore be merciful, just as your Father also is merciful. 37 "Judge not, and you shall not be judged. Condemn not, and you shall not be condemned. **Forgive, and you will be forgiven."***

1. In this passage Jesus teaches how to protect yourself from strife in all areas of your life. It is designed to keep you connected with the power of God so you can live an overcoming life. The Bible says we are more than conquerors that we are the head not the tail.

2. Love stops the work and effect of strife by building a protective shield around you.

## 5:18 Amplified Bible, Classic Edition

*18 We know [absolutely] that anyone born of God does not [deliberately and knowingly] practice committing sin, but the One Who was begotten of God carefully watches over and protects him [Christ's divine presence within him preserves him against the evil], and the wicked one does not lay hold (get a grip) on him or touch [him].*

1. **2 Timothy 2:24-26** *says the servant of the Lord must not strive but minister to those that oppose him so that God will forgive them. So that, they may recover themselves from the "snare of the devil" who takes them captive at his will.*

B. **Luke 6:38** *"Give, and it will be given to you: good measure, pressed down, shaken together, and running over will be put into your bosom. For with the same measure that you use, it will be measured back to you."*

1. **Only after presenting how to stay out of strife does**

He present the chief principle of prosperity.

2.  **Your giving will not work properly until you follow the other rules.**

3.  **1 Corinthians 13:1-3** *"Though I speak with the tongues of men and of angels, but have not love, I have become sounding brass or a clanging cymbal. 2 and though I have the gift of prophecy, and understand all mysteries and all knowledge, and though I have all faith, so that I could remove mountains, but have not love, I am nothing. 3 And though I bestow all my goods to feed the poor, and though I give my body to be burned, but have not love, it profits me nothing."* (Without love, your giving will be of no profit even if you give your life)

# Chapter 8
# You can walk in The Blessing

## Proverbs 10:22

## You are BLESSED by the BLESSOR to be a BLESSING!

**Note: The notes in chapter eight have come from many different sources. I want to give thanks to Mark Hankins, Kenneth Hagin, Jerry Savelle, Kenneth Copeland, Nancy & Ed Dufrense. Travis Peters and many other ministers who have taught and shared about The Blessing. Their teachings have helped me to increase and have an abundance God's Way.**

*"The blessing of the Lord makes one rich, and He adds no sorrow with it." –Proverbs 10:22 (NKJV)*

Do you feel like you are working and struggling to achieve your dreams?

You are not meant to do all the work!

Find out how THE BLESSING will get you there.

### Matthew 5:2-10 Amplified Bible

*2 Then He began to teach them, saying, 3 "Blessed [spiritually prosperous, happy, to be admired] are the poor in spirit [those devoid of spiritual arrogance, those who regard themselves as insignificant], for theirs is the kingdom of heaven [both now and forever].*

*4 "Blessed [forgiven, refreshed by God's grace] are those who mourn [over their sins and repent], for they will be comforted [when the burden of sin is lifted]. 5 "Blessed [inwardly peaceful, spiritually secure, worthy of respect] are the gentle [the kind-hearted, the sweet-spirited, the self-controlled], for they will inherit the earth.*

*6 "Blessed [joyful, nourished by God's goodness] are those who hunger and thirst for righteousness [those who actively seek right standing with God], for they will be [completely] satisfied. 7 "Blessed [content, sheltered by God's promises] are the merciful, for they will receive mercy. 8 "Blessed [anticipating God's presence, spiritually mature] are the pure in heart [those with integrity, moral courage, and godly character], for they will see God. 9 "Blessed [spiritually calm with life-joy in God's favor] are the makers and maintainers of peace, for they will [express His character and] b e called the sons of God. 10 "Blessed [comforted by inner peace and God's love] are those who are persecuted for doing that which is morally right, for theirs is the kingdom of heaven [both now and forever].*

Toiling and working, working, and toiling. Does that sound like your life? Sometimes it can feel like you are spinning your wheels and getting nowhere. Many people are struggling to advance but they face setback after setback, or they simply stay in the same place year after year.

**You work, but you never get ahead**!

Certainly, there is an adversary (satan) who is always ready and willing to throw hindrances your way, but what if increase and advancement could be achieved with a simple change in your thinking?

Prosperity must start in your mind, the way you think. Poverty is a mindset we must change if we want to walk in God's prosperity and abundance. We are programmed from a small child to fail and to think small. The first words we hear and learn are: "No", :You Can't", "We Can't Afford That".

**God established The BLESSING of the Lord, to enforce all your covenant rights and advance you along in life**. It was established from the very beginning with Abraham.

Sometimes it can be tempting to switch over to the flesh and try to take the reins yourself. The unintended consequence ends up in delay and frustration. We lose favor that may have come your way.

1. God has put in each one of us the instinct to work hard.

2. But we must balance our own work with a submission to the supernatural.

3. If you are ready to stop running, struggling, and toiling to reach your dreams, goals, and vision and if you begin to change your thinking with these five ways to put THE BLESSING to work in your life, your life will change for the better.

4. One way I changed the poverty mindset in my life was to make a list of things that are important in my life and prioritize them.

   1. Faith

   2. Family

   3. Finances

   4. Fulfillment

   5. Fitness

(And in this order) I learned to make a point to do something every day in these five areas to increase and make my life and the ones around me better. You should learn to keep a journal of your blessings and the success that God brings to you.

## WHAT DOES IT MEAN TO BE RICH/ WHAT IS YOUR DEFINITION OF RICH?

**1.Let THE BLESSING Make You Rich**

**Is the Bible the true inspired Word of God? We must believe that for any of this to work or even matter.**

*"The blessing of the Lord makes one rich, and He adds no sorrow with it."* **Proverbs 10:22 (NKJV)**

In this verse, that word translated *sorrow* means **"to toil."**

Now, there is nothing wrong with work. The Bible says, "If you don't work, you don't eat"

**(2 Thessalonians 3:10, *MSG).***

Work is a requirement for advancement, and the Bible is clear that diligence is required for promotion, increase and wealth. **However, there is a difference between work and toil.**

Work is putting your hands to something, so God can prosper and increase you (**Deuteronomy 28:8**).

Toil is taking the responsibility and pressure of provision onto yourself. Some Christians have argued, " I have to earn a living." There are people who will always be poor and broke. They are not willing to change their mindset and their daily habits. They will toil for all they have. The Bible teaches we must work. There is a difference in work and toiling.

**We have a saying in the US "If it is to be it is up to me!" This is not a true statement.**

Kenneth Copeland says this concerning this statement.:

"Did you earn your salvation? No. You got it by grace and through faith.

Did you earn the baptism in the Holy Ghost? How did you get it? Free gift.

Did you earn healing? How did you get that? By believing.

If you felt that you had to do something, to work or beg

God, that is what makes you think you must earn your money?" Prosperity is a free gift, but there is a spiritual law that will require you and me to go through the process. We work, we give, we tithe, we sow and God gives the rewards and increase. Obedience, patience, being willing, tithing, sowing, working, waiting, speaking… is all part of the process.

**Everything God has for the believer is free to the believer if he/she will use their faith to get it. We must be willing and obedient through the process. It will take a great discipline and discipleship to keep it**. But when we go through the process, by faith and by our works, we will eat the good of the land.

You must rely on and understand that it is a part of the blessing. It has already been made available to you and me.

The blessing of the Lord is a free gift; you should expect His blessing in your life. You need to work, but you do not need to make your own living. If you gather it for yourself, it works like a bag with holes in it.

The Bible says we work to give! That alone should be exciting for you and me.

**THE BLESSING of the Lord is what makes you rich —** *He* **makes you rich**. The more you study, the more you'll realize that THE BLESSING of the Lord is the **Glory of the Lord, is The Spirit of the Lord, is the Lord Himself. He** *is* **THE BLESSING**. Repeat that over and over to yourself until it becomes real to you.

You do not have to toil to be rich.

**If a person is on assignment for Jesus, then that person does not live on his or her salary alone.**

Each year when his board of directors determines his salary, <u>Jerry Savelle</u> — after thanking them — makes a personal declaration saying, "My salary is not my income. God is the source of my income, and my income will far exceed my salary."

The same is true for you. You are called to work, but not to struggle or toil.

**How do you do this?**

You do your work as working for the Lord, and you shift your mindset over to believing your income will far exceed your salary because God, not your salary, is your Source.

You begin to rest and not worry about your finances, You give your financial cares over to the Lord.

Jesus went to great lengths to secure THE BLESSING for you. You can be made rich and become a BLESSING to the world around you. Don't blow it by your doubt and unbelief.

**His intention is for you to be made wealthy, not just for your own enjoyment, but for the advancement of the gospel of Jesus Christ.**

When you prosper, you can bring THE BLESSING to the dark places of the world around you. Wealthy believers are satan's worst nightmare. They fund ministries, they support missionaries, and they pay off houses and cars. Satan will do everything possible to deceive you, to discourage you and cause you to give up before you receive your blessing.

You may come across someone in need, maybe a single mom who is struggling and needs food or clothing for her kids. You are living in THE BLESSING, you don't just sit there, you buy what she needs! That is why now is the time to become BLESSING-minded and know that it isn't your job, but THE BLESSING, which will make you rich! I remember for several years I would take a $10 or a $20 bill and go to a grocery store and slip those bills in the top of a can of baby formula or a box of pampers. This was just one way I blessed people. My wife and I always give more than expected when we leave a tip. We tip everyone, waiters/waitress, hairdressers, massage therapists, mechanics etc.....You may be thinking, those people make enough, they don't need my tip. You don't know that and the tipping and giving is not really for them, but for your benefit!

**It is not the place of the government to take care of the poor and needy! It is the place of the church (you and me) the believer to bless the poor.**

**Are you doing your part? Are you a part of the problem? Or are you a part of the blessing?**

**God can qualify you in the supernatural. He will give you abilities you or no one else even knew you had. When we begin to understand and walk in these abilities, God can and will promote you. He will raise you above your peers.**

**God will never make you take a position you do not want and/or are not qualified for.**

## 2. Let THE BLESSING Promote You

*"The houses will be richly stocked with goods you did not produce. You will draw water from cisterns you did not dig, and you will eat from vineyards and olive trees you did not plant." –**Deuteronomy 6:11** (NLT)*

So many times, Christians feel the need to fight their way to the top. We should float our way to the top by our generosity.

There are even some who are willing to vote with those who promote immorality to protect their Social Security, or other social programs that promote sin and wrong doings. This is a major problem in our society today. People have come to expect everything they want to be free. They expect everything to be given to them without working, without tithing, giving or sowing. Life for many people has become "it's about me and my four and no more!"

Sometimes social programs, or anything else they feel will help them advance in life becomes the main focus in people's lives, including many Christians.. **But God put THE BLESSING in place, so we do not have to toil, struggle, or rely on man to be promoted in any area of our lives. We work, we study God's Word, we act and speak according to the Word. The Word will work for us.**

**THE BLESSING will promote you even when you are not qualified in the natural.**

A. It will promote you when the world says you are not enough.

B. It will promote you when you have had one setback after another.

C. It will promote you when you are surrounded by enemies who want to keep you from ever reaching your destination.

**But you must let THE BLESSING do the work.**

When you are operating in the natural, you edge out the supernatural because you're putting the energy of your faith toward yourself, rather than toward God. When we learn to step back and stop fighting in our own strength, we can allow God to promote us. We will see advancements we never dreamed possible.

**Example:** Many years ago, I was doing mission work in the jungles and rivers of Guyana South America. One morning as we were traveling in the black rivers deep in the jungle, I was having a conversation (more like a pity party) with God.

I was crying and said, Lord why am I here in this boat (I

cannot swim). Why am I here preaching and teaching the gospel when there are so many more people more qualified than me?

I have no money and I do not know why you would even try to use me! There are better preachers and teachers. There are many more people qualified for this assignment.

The Lord listened and then He spoke to me in that soft quiet voice and said, "I have asked many to come do what you are doing, and they said no. I asked you and you said yes, Lord, send me."

He said "when you said yes, Lord, that qualified you." That is when I realized the meaning of the scripture that says (many are called but few are chosen).

All are called but you can only be chosen and qualified when you say yes, Lord, send me. Everything changed that morning and it has never been the same.

God will always qualify the called and the obedient. He will supply every need according to His riches in glory. We just have to be willing and obedient.

As Kenneth Copeland says, "THE BLESSING will make a somebody out of nobody."

That is what happened to Joseph when he was given a dream and vision for his life. That dream all but died right there in the pit where his brothers threw him. There was nothing he could do to promote himself out of that situation.

**But THE BLESSING was there**, that is what kept his brothers from killing him.

**THE BLESSING** is what sent that caravan from Egypt. They were at the right place, at the right time, to fish him out of his pit and off to his destiny.

God has a plan for your life. It is a life of blessing and abundance with no sorrow added to it.

Let me ask you a question. Are you in a pit today? Have you been stuck in a place where there looks as if there is no way out and no possibility of advancement? Take a step back and invite God into your situation. Stop trying to make something happen. Let THE BLESSING do the work and promote you to positions you are not qualified for in the natural world. (Remember God does not operate in the natural but the supernatural.) To get you houses that have always seemed out of your price range. To get you into ministries that seemed so far off. To fix your relationships you could never establish on your own. To do the impossible in your life and make it possible.

Joseph was in a situation where he could do nothing on his own. He was a slave and then a prisoner, **but the Bible says,** *"The Lord was with Joseph so that he prospered"* (**Genesis 39:2, NIV**).

He made Joseph rich and added no sorrow to it. God had to prosper Joseph to be able to bring the riches to him so that he would be able to help his brothers, his father, family, and nation during a time of famine.

God has a plan to prosper you, also, and bring you into a land of milk and honey. If we are always operating from miracle to miracle there is a problem. We are to operate from victory to victory. God will work miracles for us but we should not be living a life waiting on one miracle after another.

It does not say Joseph prospered because of his race, his influential family, his education, his social status, or his intelligence. No, **THE BLESSING** is what made Joseph prosper and receive a promotion to the second most powerful position in the world. **THE BLESSING** of the Lord does not care where you are or where you came from. The blessing works anywhere anytime for anyone that will work it according to God's Word. Stop fighting the world and try to prove yourself. Let **THE BLESSING** (Jesus) promote you, and you will find yourself in a palace, in a place of peace and prosperity!

### 3. Let THE BLESSING Defend You.

*"The Lord is your mighty defender."* –**Deuteronomy 32:4** *(GNT)*

*3 For I proclaim the name of the LORD:*
*Ascribe greatness to our God.*
*4 **He is the Rock, His work is perfect;***
*  **For all His ways are justice**,*
*A God of truth and without injustice;*
*Righteous and upright is He.* **Deuteronomy 32:3-4**

When you have been wronged, slighted or downright betrayed, do you spring into action to defend yourself?

When you have been wronged, it can be tempting to rise and take action, and sometimes the Lord will tell you to do just that. However, you should not defend yourself without His backing. WE ALL DO! Our natural nature says let ME do it and our Spiritual Man says, no let God do this. God will let us override Him, He will never make us do anything we don't want to do.

Joseph never defended himself against Potiphar.

He did not spend time fighting to get out of prison.

He waited, and he let **THE BLESSING** take care of it.

It did not happen overnight, but God avenged him in every way possible. There is no defender greater than our God. You do not have to fight your own fight. You don't have to defend yourself and look out for your own rights. If you humble yourself and step out of the way, **THE BLESSING** will go ahead of you and prepare a table before you in the presence of your enemies. The Blesser will be the best friend, boss, business partner you will ever have, but you have to submit to Him.

This is an important lesson to learn because when you walk in **THE BLESSING**, you will be persecuted. **PEOPLE WILL BE JEALOUS**

You may have a hundredfold return, with houses and lands that come from **THE BLESSING**, *along with* persecutions (**Mark 10:30**).

**THE BLESSING** on you will make people envious of you, and they will persecute you. But do not pay any attention to it. Clothe yourself with humility. Cast your cares over on Jesus. When you put the situation that has concerned you into His hands and say to Him, "Lord, will You take care of this for me?" He says, "Of course I will!"

### 4. Let THE BLESSING Anoint You.

*"His anointing teaches you about all things." – 1 John 2:27 (NIV)*

*These things I have written to you concerning those who try to deceive you.* <sup>27</sup> *<u>But the anointing which you have received from Him abides in you</u>, and you do not need that anyone teach you; but as the same anointing teaches you concerning all things, and is true, and is not a lie, and just as it has taught you, you will abide in Him.* **1 John 2:26-27**

### You don't have to have it all figured out.

This depends on your personality type, which will either be easy or tough to handle! Have you ever run up against a situation and thought, *this is hopeless,* or *I will never be able to do that*? Well, think again. No situation is hopeless when you factor in the anointing. It is ok to be taught by good teachers, and read books by godly authors that have been anointed by God for that purpose. But make sure what they teach or write does not go against what the Bible says. It should line up with what the Holy Spirit teaches and tells you. Anything that contradicts the Word of God is not of God.

**ALL THINGS ARE POSSIBLE WITH GOD.**

**THE BLESSING IS ANOTHER TOOL IN YOUR SPIRITUAL TOOLBOX.**

The anointing factor is the very power of God at work in your situation. It is God doing those things in your life that only God can do. When your mind and flesh try to take over in these situations, you soon realize, **I just do not have the strength. I do not have what it takes to combat this thing and win against it.** That is when you can step back and allow the power of God in your spirit, the anointing to take over. We should always seek His advice from the start. Come to Him when you have exhausted all your natural options and abilities, if not before!

**THE BLESSING** will anoint you to fight your battles and prosper even in a famine.

**THE ANOINTING HELPS PLAN, PREPARE, PROSPER AND BRING PEACE.**

**BEGIN TO PARTICAPATE IN WHAT GOD IS DOING IN YOUR LIFE.**

**PLAN AND BE PRECISE AND PERSISTENT IN ALL THAT YOU DO.**

Think about it—how did Joseph know how to run a ranch and a wealthy man's property?

**THE BLESSING** of the Lord gave him the mind of God, the mind of the Holy Spirit. As born-again believers, you and I also have been given the mind of Christ.

**THE BLESSING** anointed Joseph, this made Potiphar rich, and then made Pharaoh the richest man in the world.

**VIP:** The same anointing that was on the mind of Jesus when He was ministering on this earth is the same anointing available to you right now. **But it must be obtained and released by faith, and Love through FAITH**. You are anointed! It is the same anointing that was on Joseph's life.

That is why Abraham was so strong in faith, **He was BLESSED!** He learned how to receive and how to depend on **THE BLESSING**. As long as he depended on it, it didn't matter where he dug a hole, he hit water. God's plan always works to the benefit of the one who believes and then acts on what he/she believes.

People will always tell you why you cannot do something. But once you find out the will of God for you, do not operate in the flesh. You can began to operate in the supernatural. When I was praying about the plan for my life. I had a man that I considered a faith person, and a mentor tell me I could not do what I believed God was telling me to do. He said it won't work, you can't raise the money. I was told all the negative reason I should not do what I believed to be God's plan for me. I left his office disappointed. But I knew I had heard the voice of the Lord about His plan for my life. I believed and began to act and pray as if it were already in motion. God worked miracle after miracle. That was 21 years ago and it is still working as God had said it would. I am in my 29th year of ministry and very thankful I did not listen to the negative voice that said, "You can't, you won't, you can't raise the money." When the blessing is on your life, walk in it to its fullness. No one's opinion is better or more powerful than God's plan.

Let **THE BLESSING** take you where no one thinks you can go.

**THE BLESSING** will bring you revelation knowledge. It is the gateway to the supernatural.

When you are facing a situation, a goal or a job that requires anointing, don't wear yourself out. Don't overwork your brain hour after hour, searching every nook and cranny for the answer.

If you knew what to do, it would not be a trial. So, count it all joy, and sit down in God's rest, believing His wisdom is on the way.

You have a covenant right to expect the power of God in your life to work on your behalf. Factor in the power of God's Word. Factor in the power of His Spirit. Factor in the Anointing. **Let THE BLESSING do the work and watch those circumstances change!**

**6.Let THE BLESSING Preach the Gospel.**

**THE BLESSING IS GOOD NEWS**

*"I came that they may have life and have it abundantly." –John 10:10 (ESV)*

*The thief does not come except to **steal**, and to **kill**, and to **destroy**. I have come that they may have life, and that they may have it more abundantly. John 10:10 NKJV*

It's fun to talk about the ways **THE BLESSING** can make us rich, promote us, defend us and anoint us, but above all, **THE BLESSING** preaches the gospel to a lost world. **VIP**

When you are living in **THE BLESSING**, you aren't spending your time worrying or toiling. You have the time, energy, money and anointing to minister to others. You're an example of what it looks like to be a child of the Most High God. When you are walking and living in **THE BLESSING**, you shine a light in a dark world. People will naturally be drawn to you, they will want what you have! Everyone wants to BE BLESSED, and you will know how to help them get there.

**THE BLESSING** is the gospel of Jesus Christ! Take it and be a witness as He is called you to do.

It is time to put **THE BLESSING** to work in every area of your life! Any area of your life where you have been held back, there's only one thing missing — **THE BLESSING**.

No more toiling, no more struggling, no more standing in a defensive posture. No more guesswork, let **THE BLESSING** do the work for you!

We are **BLESSED**. The Bible is full of verses saying just that. Jesus paid the price **for everything** we could ever need or desire now and for eternity. Yet so many Christians are crying out to God and acting like He has not already provided for them. Instead of begging God to BLESS us, what we ought to be doing is developing our faith in what He has already done for us. We should be meditating on what the Bible says about who we are and **THE BLESSING** that is on us, so that we become aware of it all the time.

We should be thinking about it every day, putting it on 3-by-5-inch cards on the refrigerator, walls and on our bathroom mirrors to remind ourselves of it, and constantly saying to ourselves: "**I am as BLESSED** as Adam was before the Fall.

**I am as BLESSED as Abraham was.**

**I am as BLESSED as Jesus is.**

**I am BLESSED to be a Blessing!"**

When you catch a revelation of what **THE BLESSING** has done and is doing for you, your life will never be the same.

Allow the Word of God to convert your thinking, fuel your faith, and accomplish God's will for your life.

**Failure is not an option!**

Set yourself on the path to guaranteed success today with these 10 scriptures about the power of **THE BLESSING** in every area of your life!

**Ten Scriptures for THE BLESSING**

1. *"BLESSED be the God and Father of our Lord Jesus Christ, who has BLESSED us [past tense!] with every spiritual BLESSING in the heavenly places in Christ, just as He chose us in Him before the foundation of the world, that we should be holy and without blame before Him in love."* –**Ephesians 1:3-4** *(NKJV)*

2. *"Christ has redeemed us from the curse of the law, having become a curse for us (for it is written, 'Cursed is everyone who hangs on a tree'), that* **THE BLESSING** *of Abraham might come upon the Gentiles in Christ Jesus, that we might receive the promise of the Spirit through faith."* –**Galatians 3:13-14** *(NKJV)*

3. *"Then God BLESSED them, and God said to them, 'Be fruitful and multiply; fill the earth and subdue it; have dominion over the fish of the sea, over the birds of the air, and over every living thing that moves on the earth.'"* –**Genesis 1:28** *(NKJV)*

4. *"For You, O Lord, will BLESS the righteous; with favor You will surround him as with a shield."* –**Psalm 5:12** *(NKJV)*

5. *"For whatever is born of God* **[THE BLESSING]** *overcomes the world. And this is the victory that has overcome the world — our faith."* –**1 John 5:4** *(NKJV)*

6. *"Therefore it is of faith that it might be according to grace, so that* **the promise** *[of* **THE BLESSING***] might be sure to all the seed, not only to those who are of the law, but also to those who are of the faith of Abraham, who is the father of us all."* –**Romans 4:16** *(NKJV)*

7. *"Now it shall come to pass, if you diligently obey the voice of the Lord your God, to observe carefully all His commandments which I command you today, that the Lord your God will set you high above*

*all nations of the earth. And all these blessings shall come upon you and overtake you, because you obey the voice of the Lord your God:* **BLESSED** *shall you be in the city, and blessed shall you be in the country.* **BLESSED** *shall be the fruit of your body, the produce of your ground and the increase of your herds, the increase of your cattle and the offspring of your flocks.* **BLESSED** *shall be your basket and your kneading bowl.* **BLESSED** *shall you be when you come in, and blessed shall you be when you go out. 'The Lord will cause your enemies who rise against you to be defeated before your face; they shall come out against you one way and flee before you seven ways. 'The Lord will command* **THE BLESSING** *on you in your storehouses and in all to which you set your hand, and He will* **BLESS** *you in the land which the Lord your God is giving you.'"* – **Deuteronomy 28:1-8**

8. *"Then God said, 'Let us make human beings in our image, to be like us. They will reign over the fish in the sea, the birds in the sky, the livestock, all the wild animals on the earth, and the small animals that scurry along the ground.' So, God created human beings in his own image. In the image of God, he created them; male and female he created them. Then God* **BLESSED** *them and said, 'Be fruitful and multiply. Fill the earth and govern it. Reign over the fish in the sea, the birds in the sky, and all the animals that scurry along the ground.'"* — **Genesis 1:26-28**

9. **"THE BLESSING** *of the Lord makes one rich, and He adds no sorrow with it."* –**Proverbs 10:22**

10. *"***Bless** *the Lord, O my soul, and forget not all His benefits: who forgives all your iniquities, who heals all your diseases, who redeems your life from destruction, who crowns you with loving kindness and tender mercies, who satisfies your mouth with good things, so that your youth is renewed like the eagle's."* –**Psalm 103:2-5**

We are **BLESSED**! It is time we, as believers, started acting as if those verses are true. It is time we stopped going before the Lord in prayer saying, "Oh God, please **BLESS** me!" That is an absolute waste of breath because we are already **BLESSED**.

We are as **BLESSED** as we can be. Set aside some time to meditate on these verses, even if it is just a few minutes a day. Obey Jesus. Think about the ravens and how God feeds them. Think about how much more you mean to your Heavenly Father than the birds. Kick out the thoughts of how little you are worth.

Jesus loves you and gave Himself for you (**Galatians 2:20**). Fix that in your heart and mind. Do not put it off! Do it now.

Talk about it to yourself. Then reach out to someone.

Do something to **BLESS** someone. Let the truth about the power of **THE BLESSING** become more real to you than anything else in your life!

# Chapter 9
# Financial/Prosperity Scriptures For Your Personal Studies.

## Genesis

### Genesis 1:26-28 Amplified Bible, Classic Edition

*26 God said, Let Us [Father, Son, and Holy Spirit] make mankind in Our image, after Our likeness, and let them have complete authority over the fish of the sea, the birds of the air, the [tame] beasts, and over all of the earth, and over everything that creeps upon the earth.27 So God created man in His own image, in the image and likeness of God He created him; male and female He created them.28 **And God blessed them and said to them, Be fruitful, multiply, and fill the earth, and subdue it [using all its vast resources in the service of God and man]; and have dominion over the fish of the sea, the birds of the air, and over every living creature that moves upon the earth.***

---

### Genesis 2:8 New King James Version

### Life in God's Garden

*8 The Lord God planted a garden eastward in Eden, and there He put the man whom He had formed.*

*DRA*

*And the Lord God had planted a paradise of pleasure from the beginning: wherein he placed man whom he had formed.*

---

*Genesis 8:22 Amplified Bible, Classic Edition*

²² *While the earth remains, seedtime and harvest, cold and heat, summer and winter, and day and night shall not cease.*

---

## Genesis 15:1 Amplified Bible, Classic Edition

¹⁵ *After these things, the word of the Lord came to Abram in a vision, saying, Fear not, Abram, I am your Shield,* **your abundant compensation, and your reward shall be exceedingly great.**

---

## Genesis 17:1-9 Amplified Bible, Classic Edition

*17 When Abram was ninety-nine years old, the Lord appeared to him and said, I am the Almighty God; walk and live habitually before Me and be perfect (blameless, wholehearted, complete). ² And I will make My covenant (solemn pledge) between Me and you and will multiply you exceedingly. ³ Then Abram fell on his face, and God said to him, ⁴ As for Me, behold, My covenant (solemn pledge) is with you, and you shall be the father of many nations. ⁵ Nor shall your name any longer be Abram [high, exalted father]; but your name shall be Abraham [father of a multitude], for I have made you the father of many nations. ⁶ And I will make you exceedingly fruitful and I will make nations of you, and kings will come from you.* **⁷ And I will establish My covenant between Me and you and your descendants after you throughout their generations for an everlasting, solemn pledge, to be a God to you and to your posterity after you.** *⁸ And I will give to you and to your posterity after you the land in which you are a stranger [going from place to place], all the land of Canaan, for an everlasting possession; and I will be their God. ⁹ And God said to Abraham, As for you, you shall therefore keep My covenant, you and your descendants after you throughout their generations.*

---

## Genesis 24:1 Amplified Bible, Classic Edition

*24 Now Abraham was old, well advanced in years, and the Lord had blessed Abraham in all things.*

---

## Genesis 25:8 Amplified Bible, Classic Edition

*8 Then Abraham's spirit was released, and he died at a good (ample, full) old age, an old man, satisfied and satiated, and was gathered to his people.*

---

## Genesis 26:13-14 Amplified Bible, Classic Edition

*13 And the man became great and gained more and more until he became very wealthy and distinguished; 14 He owned flocks, herds, and a great supply of servants, and the Philistines envied him.*

---

## Genesis 26:24 Amplified Bible, Classic Edition

*24 And the Lord appeared to him the same night and said, I am the God of Abraham your father. Fear not, for I am with you and will favor you with blessings and multiply your descendants for the sake of My servant Abraham.*

---

## Genesis 30:43 Amplified Bible, Classic Edition

*43 Thus the man increased and became exceedingly rich, and had many sheep and goats, and maidservants, menservants, camels, and donkeys.*

---

## Genesis 31:7-12 Amplified Bible, Classic Edition

*7 But your father has deceived me and changed my wages ten times, but God did not allow him to hurt me. 8 If he said, The speckled shall be your wages, then all the flock bore speckled; and if he said, The streaked shall be your hire, then all the flock bore streaked. 9 Thus God has taken away the flocks of your father and given them to me. 10 And I had a dream at the time the flock conceived. I looked up and saw that the rams which mated with the she-goats were streaked, speckled, and spotted. 11 And the Angel of God said to me in the dream, Jacob. And I said, Here am I. 12 And He said, Look up and see, all the rams which mate with the flock are streaked, speckled, and mottled; for I have seen all that Laban does to you.*

### Footnotes

*Genesis 31:10 We naturally wonder why we have not heard of this dream before and are tempted to question Jacob's truthfulness; but the Samaritan text removes all such doubt by recording the whole dream in the previous chapter (Gen. 30), right after Gen. 30:36 (Adam Clarke, The Holy Bible with A Commentary).*

*Genesis 31:11 See footnote on Gen. 16:7. Note especially Gen. 31:13, where the Angel says, "I am the God of Bethel."*

---

## Genesis 35:29 Amplified Bible, Classic Edition

*29 And Isaac's spirit departed; he died and was gathered to his people, being an old man, satisfied and satiated with days; his sons Esau and Jacob buried him.*

---

## Genesis 39:2-3 Amplified Bible, Classic Edition

*2 But the Lord was with Joseph, and he [though a slave] was a successful and prosperous man; and he was in the house of his master the Egyptian. 3 And his master saw that the Lord was with him and that the Lord made all that he did to flourish and succeed in his hand.*

---

## Genesis 39:21-23 Amplified Bible, Classic Edition

*But the Lord was with Joseph and showed him mercy and loving-kindness and gave him favor in the sight of the warden of the prison. 22 And the warden of the prison committed to Joseph's care all the prisoners who were in the prison; and whatsoever was done there, he was in charge of it. 23 The prison warden paid no attention to anything that was in [Joseph's] charge, for the Lord was with him and made whatever he did to prosper.*

---

## Genesis 41:42-43 Amplified Bible, Classic Edition

*42 And Pharaoh took off his [signet] ring from his hand and put it on Joseph's hand, and arrayed him in [official] vestments of fine linen and put a gold chain about his neck; 43 He made him to ride in the second chariot which he had, and [officials] cried before him, Bow the knee! And he set him over all the land of Egypt.*

---

## Deuteronomy

## Deuteronomy 6:3 Amplified Bible, Classic Edition

*3 Hear therefore, O Israel, and be watchful to do them, that it may be well with you and that you may increase exceedingly, as the Lord, the God of your fathers, has promised you, in a land flowing with milk and honey.*

---

## Deuteronomy 6:10-12 Amplified Bible, Classic Edition

*10 And when the Lord your God brings you into the land which He swore to your fathers, to Abraham, Isaac, and Jacob, to give you, with great and goodly cities which you did not build, 11 And houses full of all good things which you did not fill, and cisterns hewn out which you did not hew, and vineyards and olive trees which you did not plant, and when you eat and are full, 12 Then beware lest you forget the Lord, Who brought you out of the land of Egypt, out of the house of bondage.*

---

## Deuteronomy 8:17-18 Amplified Bible, Classic Edition

*And beware lest you say in your [mind and] heart, My power and the might of my hand have gotten me this wealth.* **[18] But you shall [earnestly] remember the Lord your God, for it is He Who gives you power to get wealth, that He may establish His covenant which He swore to your fathers, as it is this day.**

---

## Deuteronomy 14:23 Amplified Bible, Classic Edition

*[23] And you shall eat before the Lord your God in the place in which He will cause His Name [and Presence] to dwell the tithe (tenth) of your grain, your new wine, your oil, and the firstlings of your herd and your flock, that you may learn [reverently] to fear the Lord your God always.*

---

## Deuteronomy 26:8-9 Amplified Bible, Classic Edition

*[8] And the Lord brought us forth out of Egypt with a mighty hand and with an outstretched arm, and with great (awesome) power and with signs and with wonders; [9] And He brought us into this place and gave us this land, a land flowing with milk and honey.*

---

## Deuteronomy 28:8-11 Amplified Bible, Classic Edition

*[8] The Lord shall command the blessing upon you in your storehouse and in all that you undertake. And He will bless you in the land which the Lord your God gives you. [9] The Lord will establish you as a people holy to Himself, as He has sworn to you, if you keep the commandments of the Lord your God and walk in His ways. [10] And all people of the earth shall see that you are called by the name [and in the*

*presence of] the Lord, and they shall be afraid of you.*[11] *And the Lord shall make you have a surplus of prosperity, through the fruit of your body, of your livestock, and of your ground, in the land which the Lord swore to your fathers to give you.*

---

## Deuteronomy 28:29-30 Amplified Bible, Classic Edition

[29] *And you shall grope at noonday as the blind grope in darkness. And you shall not prosper in your ways; and you shall be only oppressed and robbed continually, and there shall be no one to save you.*[30] *You shall betroth a wife, but another man shall lie with her; you shall build a house, but not live in it; you shall plant a vineyard, but not gather its grapes.* [33] *A nation which you have not known shall eat up the fruit of your land and of all your labors, and you shall be only oppressed and crushed continually,* [**Fulfilled in Judg. 6:1-6; 13:1.**] [44] *He shall lend to you, but you shall not lend to him; he shall be the head, and you shall be the tail.*

---

## Deuteronomy 29:9 Amplified Bible, Classic Edition

[9] *Therefore keep the words of this covenant and do them, that you may deal wisely and prosper in all that you do.*

---

## Deuteronomy 30:19 Amplified Bible, Classic Edition

[19] *I call heaven and earth to witness this day against you that I have set before you life and death, the blessings and the curses; therefore choose life, that you and your descendants may live.*

---

## Leviticus

## Leviticus 27:30 Amplified Bible, Classic Edition

[30] *And all the tithe of the land, whether of the seed of the land or of*

*the fruit of the tree, is the Lord's; it is holy to the Lord.*

---

## Joshua 1:8 Amplified Bible, Classic Edition

*8 This Book of the Law shall not depart out of your mouth, but you shall meditate on it day and night, that you may observe and do according to all that is written in it. For then you shall make your way prosperous, and then you shall deal wisely and have good [a]success.*

### Footnotes

*Joshua 1:8 This is the only place in the early English versions where the word "success" is found. The secret of success is given in verses 5 through 9. Joshua accepted Moses' place of leadership without misgivings. God's will for him was his will, and he did not hesitate. To go "all out" for God was already habitual with him; it is the unfailing prerequisite of eternal success (Deut. 6:3-5; Ps. 1:1-3; Luke 10:25-28).*

---

## 1st Chronicles

## 1 Chronicles 29:3 New King James Version

*3 Moreover, because I have set my affection on the house of my God, I have given to the house of my God, over and above all that I have prepared for the holy house, my own special treasure of gold and silver:*

*ASV.*

*Moreover also, because I have set my affection on the house of my God, seeing that I have a treasure of mine own of gold and silver, I give it unto the house of my God, over and above all that I have prepared for the holy house,*

*MSG.*

*Then David the king addressed the congregation: "My son*

*Solomon was singled out and chosen by God to do this. But he's young and untested and the work is huge — this is not just a place for people to meet each other, but a house for GOD to meet us. I've done my best to get everything together for building this house for my God, all the materials necessary: gold, silver, bronze, iron, lumber, precious and varicolored stones, and building stones — vast stockpiles. Furthermore, because my heart is in this, in addition to and beyond what I have gathered, I'm turning over my personal fortune of gold and silver for making this place of worship for my God: 3,000 talents (about 113 tons) of gold — all from Ophir, the best — and 7,000 talents (214 tons) of silver for covering the walls of the buildings, and for the gold and silver work by craftsmen and artisans. "And now, how about you? Who among you is ready and willing to join in the giving?"*

---

## 2nd Chronicles

### 2 Chronicles 20:20 New King James Version

*20 So they rose early in the morning and went out into the Wilderness of Tekoa; and as they went out, Jehoshaphat stood and said, "Hear me, O Judah and you inhabitants of Jerusalem: Believe in the LORD your God, and you shall be established; believe His prophets, and you shall prosper."*

---

### 2 Chronicles 26:5 New King James Version

*5 He sought God in the days of Zechariah, who had understanding in the visions of God; and as long as he sought the LORD, God made him prosper. sought after the LORD, God caused him to succeed.*

---

## Job

### Job 8:6-7 Amplified Bible, Classic Edition

*Then, if you are pure and upright, surely He will bestir Himself for you and make your righteous dwelling prosperous again. ⁷ And though your beginning was small, yet your latter end would greatly increase.*

---

## Job 22:28 Amplified Bible, Classic Edition

*²⁸ You shall also decide and decree a thing, and it shall be established for you; and the light [of God's favor] shall shine upon your ways.*

---

## Job 36:11 New King James Version

*¹¹ If they obey and serve Him, They shall spend their days in prosperity, And their years in pleasures.*

*AMPC If they obey and serve Him, they shall spend their days in prosperity and their years in pleasantness and joy.*

---

## Psalm

## Psalm 5:12 Amplified Bible, Classic Edition

*¹² For You, Lord, will bless the [uncompromisingly] righteous [him who is upright and in right standing with You]; as with a shield You will surround him with goodwill (pleasure and favor).*

---

## The LORD, the Psalmist's Shepherd. A Psalm of David. 23ᴿᴰ Psalm Amplified Bible

*23 The LORD is my Shepherd [to feed, to guide and to shield me], I shall not want. ² He lets me lie down in green pastures; He leads me beside the still and quiet waters.*

*KJ21. The LORD is my shepherd; I shall not want.*

*EASY. This is a song that David wrote. The LORD takes care of me, like a shepherd with his sheep. I have everything that I need.*

---

## Psalm 34:9 Amplified Bible, Classic Edition

*⁹ O fear the Lord, you His saints [revere and worship Him]! For there is no want to those who truly revere and worship Him with godly fear.*

---

## Psalm 34:10 Amplified Bible, Classic Edition

*¹⁰ The young lions lack food and suffer hunger, but they who seek (inquire of and require) the Lord [by right of their need and on the authority of His Word], none of them shall lack any beneficial thing.*

---

## Psalm 35:27 Amplified Bible, Classic Edition

*27.Let those who favor my righteous cause and have pleasure in my uprightness shout for joy and be glad and say continually, Let the Lord be magnified, Who takes pleasure in the prosperity of His servant.*

---

## Psalm 37:4 Amplified Bible, Classic Edition

*⁴ Delight yourself also in the Lord, and He will give you the desires and secret petitions of your heart.*

---

## Psalm 37:13 Amplified Bible, Classic Edition

*¹³ The Lord laughs at [the wicked], for He sees that their own day [of defeat] is coming.*

---

## Psalm 37:19 Amplified Bible, Classic Edition

*19 They shall not be put to shame in the time of evil; and in the days of famine they shall be satisfied.*

---

## Psalm 65:11 Amplified Bible, Classic Edition

*11 You crown the year with Your bounty and goodness, and the tracks of Your [chariot wheels] drip with fatness. 12 You caused men to ride over our heads [when we were prostrate]; we went through fire and through water, but You brought us out into a broad, moist place [to abundance and refreshment and the open air].*

---

## Psalm 84:11 Amplified Bible, Classic Edition

*11 For the Lord God is a Sun and Shield; the Lord bestows [present] grace and favor and [future] glory (honor, splendor, and heavenly bliss)! No good thing will He withhold from those who walk uprightly.*

---

## Psalm 92:13 Amplified Bible, Classic Edition

*13 Planted in the house of the Lord, they shall flourish in the courts of our God.*

---

## Psalm 103:20-22 Amplified Bible, Classic Edition

*Bless (affectionately, gratefully praise) the Lord, you His angels, you mighty ones who do His commandments, hearkening to the voice of His word. 21 Bless (affectionately, gratefully praise) the Lord, all you His hosts, you His ministers who do His pleasure. 22 Bless the Lord, all His works in all places of His dominion; bless (affectionately, gratefully praise) the Lord, O my soul!*

---

## Psalm 105:37 Amplified Bible, Classic Edition

*37 He brought [Israel] forth also with silver and gold, and there was not one feeble person among their tribes.*

---

## Psalm 112 Amplified Bible, Classic Edition

*1 Praise the Lord! (Hallelujah!) Blessed (happy, fortunate, to be envied) is the man who fears (reveres and worships) the Lord, who delights greatly in His commandments. 2 His [spiritual] offspring shall be mighty upon earth; the generation of the upright shall be blessed. 3 Prosperity and welfare are in his house, and his righteousness endures forever. 4 Light arises in the darkness for the upright, gracious, compassionate, and just [who are in right standing with God]. 5 It is well with the man who deals generously and lends, who conducts his affairs with justice. 6 He will not be moved forever; the [uncompromisingly] righteous (the upright, in right standing with God) shall be in everlasting remembrance. 7 He shall not be afraid of evil tidings; his heart is firmly fixed, trusting (leaning on and being confident) in the Lord. 8 His heart is established and steady, he will not be afraid while he waits to see his desire established upon his adversaries. 9 He has distributed freely [he has given to the poor and needy]; his righteousness (uprightness and right standing with God) endures forever; his horn shall be exalted in honor. 10 The wicked man will see it and be grieved and angered, he will gnash his teeth and disappear [in despair]; the desire of the wicked shall perish and come to nothing.*

---

## Psalm 115:14 Amplified Bible, Classic Edition

*14 May the Lord give you increase more and more, you and your children.*

---

## Psalm 147:14 Amplified Bible, Classic Edition

*14 He makes peace in your borders; He fills you with the finest of the wheat.*

---

## Proverbs

### Proverbs 3:5-6 Amplified Bible, Classic Edition

*Lean on, trust in, and be confident in the Lord with all your heart and mind and do not rely on your own insight or understanding. 6 In all your ways know, recognize, and acknowledge Him, and He will direct and make straight and plain your paths.*

---

### Proverbs 3:9-10 Amplified Bible, Classic Edition

*9 Honor the Lord with your capital and sufficiency [from righteous labors] and with the first fruits of all your income;10 So shall your storage places be filled with plenty, and your vats shall be overflowing with new wine.*

---

### Proverbs 4:20-21 Amplified Bible, Classic Edition

*My son, attend to my words; consent and submit to my sayings. 21 Let them not depart from your sight; keep them in the center of your heart.*

---

### Proverbs 4:23 Amplified Bible, Classic Edition

*Keep and guard your heart with all vigilance and above all that you guard, for out of it flow the springs of life.*

---

### Proverbs 7:2 Amplified Bible, Classic Edition

*2 Keep my commandments and live, and keep my law and teaching as the apple (the pupil) of your eye.*

---

## Proverbs 8:20-21 Amplified Bible, Classic Edition

*I [Wisdom] walk in the way of righteousness (moral and spiritual rectitude in    every area and relation), in the midst of the paths of justice, 21 That I may cause those who love me to inherit [true] riches and that I may fill their treasuries.*

---

## Proverbs 10:22 Amplified Bible, Classic Edition

*The blessing of the Lord — it makes [truly] rich, and He adds no sorrow with it [neither does toiling increase it].*

---

## Proverbs 11:24-25 Amplified Bible, Classic Edition

*There are those who [generously] scatter abroad, and yet increase more; there are those who withhold more than is fitting or what is justly due, but it results only in want. 25 The liberal person shall be enriched, and he who waters shall himself be watered.*

---

## Proverbs 11:17 Amplified Bible, Classic Edition

*17 The merciful, kind, and generous man benefits himself [for his deeds return to bless him], but he who is cruel and callous [to the wants of others] brings on himself retribution.*

---

## Proverbs 11:19 Amplified Bible, Classic Edition

*19 He who is steadfast in righteousness (uprightness and right standing with God) attains to life, but he who pursues evil does it to his own death.*

## Proverbs 13:22 Amplified Bible, Classic Edition

*A good man leaves an inheritance [of moral stability and goodness] to his children's children, and the wealth of the sinner [finds its way eventually] into the hands of the righteous, for whom it was laid up.*

## Proverbs 15:6 Amplified Bible, Classic Edition

*6 In the house of the [uncompromisingly] righteous is great [priceless] treasure, but with the income of the wicked is trouble and vexation.*

## Proverbs 18:20-21 Amplified Bible, Classic Edition

*A man's [moral] self shall be filled with the fruit of his mouth; and with the consequence of his words he must be satisfied [whether good or evil]. 21 Death and life are in the power of the tongue, and they who indulge in it shall eat the fruit of it [for death or life].*

## Proverbs 22:4 Amplified Bible, Classic Edition

*4 The reward of humility and the reverent and worshipful fear of the Lord is riches and honor and life.*

## Proverbs 23:7 Amplified Bible, Classic Edition

*7 For as he thinks in his heart, so is he. As one who reckons, he says to you, eat and drink, yet his heart is not with you [but is grudging the cost.*

## Proverbs 28:10 Amplified Bible, Classic Edition

*10 Whoever leads the upright astray into an evil way, he will himself fall into his own pit, but the blameless will have a goodly inheritance.*

---

## Ecclesiastes

## Ecclesiastes 11:1-6 Amplified Bible, Classic Edition

*Cast your bread upon the waters, for you will find it after many days. 2 Give a portion to seven, yes, even [divide it] to eight, for you know not what evil may come upon the earth. 3 If the clouds are full of rain, they empty themselves upon the earth; and if a tree falls toward the south or toward the north, in the place where the tree falls, there it will lie. 4 He who observes the wind [and waits for all conditions to be favorable] will not sow, and he who regards the clouds will not reap. 5 As you know not what is the way of the wind, or how the spirit comes to the bones in the womb of a pregnant woman, even so you know not the work of God, Who does all. 6 In the morning sow your seed, and in the evening withhold not your hands, for you know not which shall prosper, whether this or that, or whether both alike will be good.*

---

## Isaiah

## Isaiah 1:19 Amplified Bible, Classic Edition

*19 If you are willing and obedient, you shall eat the good of the land;*

*ICB. If you will obey me, you will eat good crops from the land.*

---

## Isaiah 32:20 Amplified Bible, Classic Edition

*20 Happy and fortunate are you who cast your seed upon all waters [when the river overflows its banks; for the seed will sink into the mud and when the waters subside, the plant will spring up; you will find it after many days and reap an abundant harvest], you who safely send forth the ox and the donkey [to range freely].*

---

## Isaiah 48:17-18 Amplified Bible, Classic Edition

*17 Thus says the Lord, your Redeemer, the Holy One of Israel: I am the Lord your God, Who teaches you to profit, Who leads you in the way that you should go. 18 Oh, that you had hearkened to My commandments! Then your peace and prosperity would have been like a flowing river, and your righteousness [the holiness and purity of the nation] like the [abundant] waves of the sea.*

---

## Isaiah 58:14 Amplified Bible, Classic Edition

*14 Then will you delight yourself in the Lord, and I will make you to ride on the high places of the earth, and I will feed you with the heritage [promised for you] of Jacob your father; for the mouth of the Lord has spoken it.*

---

## Isaiah 54:2 Amplified Bible, Classic Edition

*2 Enlarge the place of your tent, and let the curtains of your habitations be stretched out; spare not; lengthen your cords and strengthen your stakes,*

---

## Isaiah 55:11 Amplified Bible, Classic Edition

*11 So shall My word be that goes forth out of My mouth: it shall not return to Me void [without producing any effect, useless], but it shall accomplish that which I please and purpose, and it shall prosper in the thing for which I sent it.*

---

## Isaiah 61:7 Amplified Bible, Classic Edition

*7 Instead of your [former] shame you shall have a twofold recompense; instead of dishonor and reproach [your people] shall rejoice in their portion. Therefore in their land they shall possess double [what they had forfeited]; everlasting joy shall be theirs.*

---

# Jeremiah

## Jeremiah 29:11-13 Amplified Bible, Classic Edition

*For I know the thoughts and plans that I have for you, says the Lord, thoughts and plans for welfare and peace and not for evil, to give you hope in your final outcome. 12 Then you will call upon Me, and you will come and pray to Me, and I will hear and heed you. 13 Then you will seek Me, inquire for, and require Me [as a vital necessity] and find Me when you search for Me with all your heart.*

---

# Malachi

## Malachi 3:8-12 Amplified Bible, Classic Edition

*8 Will a man rob or defraud God? Yet you rob and defraud Me. But you say, In what way do we rob or defraud You? [You have withheld your] tithes and offerings. 9 You are cursed with the curse, for you are robbing Me, even this whole nation. 10 Bring all the tithes (the whole tenth of your income) into the storehouse, that there may be food in My house, and prove Me now by it, says the Lord of hosts, if I will not open the windows of heaven for you and pour you out a blessing, that there shall not be room enough to receive it. 11 And I will rebuke the devourer [insects and plagues] for your sakes and he shall not destroy the fruits of your ground, neither shall your vine drop its fruit before the time in the field, says the Lord of hosts. 12 And all nations shall call you happy and blessed, for you shall be a land of delight, says the Lord of hosts.*

## New Testament

## Matthew

## Matthew 5:1-10 Amplified Bible, Classic Edition

*¹ Seeing the crowds, He went up on the mountain; and when He was seated, His disciples came to Him. ² Then He opened His mouth and taught them, saying: ³ Blessed (happy, to be envied, and spiritually prosperous — with life-joy and satisfaction in God's favor and salvation, regardless of their outward conditions) are the poor in spirit (the humble, who rate themselves insignificant), for theirs is the kingdom of heaven! ⁴ Blessed and enviably happy [with a happiness produced by the experience of God's favor and especially conditioned by the revelation of His matchless grace] are those who mourn, for they shall be comforted! ⁵ Blessed (happy, blithesome, joyous, spiritually prosperous — with life-joy and satisfaction in God's favor and salvation, regardless of their outward conditions) are the meek (the mild, patient, long-suffering), for they shall inherit the earth! ⁶ Blessed and fortunate and happy and spiritually prosperous (in that state in which the born-again child of God enjoys His favor and salvation) are those who hunger and thirst for righteousness (uprightness and right standing with God), for they shall be completely satisfied! ⁷ Blessed (happy, to be envied, and spiritually prosperous — with life-joy and satisfaction in God's favor and salvation, regardless of their outward conditions) are the merciful, for they shall obtain mercy! ⁸ Blessed (happy, enviably fortunate, and spiritually prosperous — possessing the happiness produced by the experience of God's favor and especially conditioned by the revelation of His grace, regardless of their outward conditions) are the pure in heart, for they shall see God! ⁹ Blessed (enjoying enviable happiness, spiritually prosperous — with life-joy and satisfaction in God's favor and salvation, regardless of their outward conditions) are the makers and maintainers of peace, for they shall be called the sons of God! ¹⁰ Blessed and happy and enviably fortunate and spiritually prosperous (in the state in which the born-again child of God enjoys and finds satisfaction in God's favor and salvation, regardless of his outward conditions) are those who are persecuted for righteousness' sake (for being and doing right), for theirs is the kingdom of heaven!*

---

## Matthew 6:1-6 Amplified Bible, Classic Edition

*6 Take care not to do your good deeds publicly or before men, in order to be seen by them; otherwise you will have no reward [reserved for and awaiting you] with and from your Father Who is in heaven. 2 Thus, whenever you give to the poor, do not blow a trumpet before you, as the hypocrites in the synagogues and in the streets like to do, that they may be recognized and honored and praised by men. Truly I tell you, they have their reward in full already. 3 But when you give to charity, do not let your left hand know what your right hand is doing, 4 So that your deeds of charity may be in secret; and your Father Who sees in secret will reward you openly. 5 Also when you pray, you must not be like the hypocrites, for they love to pray standing in the synagogues and on the corners of the streets, that they may be seen by people. Truly I tell you, they have their reward in full already. 6 But when you pray, go into your [most] private room, and, closing the door, pray to your Father, Who is in secret; and your Father, Who sees in secret, will reward you in the open.*

---

## Matthew 6:21 Amplified Bible, Classic Edition

*21 For where your treasure is, there will your heart be also.*

*AMP.*

*for where your treasure is, there your heart [your wishes, your desires; that on which your life centers] will be also.*

*EASY.*

*Then you will be thinking a lot about heaven, because that is where you keep your valuable things.*

<u>NTFE</u>.

*Show me your treasure, and I'll show you where your heart is.*

---

## Matthew 6:25-26    Amplified Bible, Classic Edition

*Therefore I tell you, stop being perpetually uneasy (anxious and worried) about your life, what you shall eat or what you shall drink; or about your body, what you shall put on. Is not life greater [in quality] than food, and the body [far above and more excellent] than clothing? 26 Look at the birds of the air; they neither sow nor reap nor gather into barns, and yet your heavenly Father keeps feeding them. Are you not worth much more than they?*

---

## Matthew 6:31-33 Amplified Bible, Classic Edition

*31 Therefore do not worry and be anxious, saying, What are we going to have to eat? or, What are we going to have to drink? or, What are we going to have to wear? 32 For the Gentiles (heathen) wish for and crave and diligently seek all these things, and your heavenly Father knows well that you need them all. 33 But seek aim at and strive after) first of all His kingdom and His righteousness His way of doing and being right), and then all these things taken together will be given you besides.*

---

## Matthew 8:2-4  Amplified Bible, Classic Edition

*2 And behold, a leper came up to Him and, prostrating himself, worshiped Him, saying, Lord, if You are willing, You are able to cleanse me by curing me. 3 And He reached out His hand and touched him, saying, I am willing; be cleansed by being cured. And instantly his leprosy was cured and cleansed. 4 And Jesus said to him, See that you tell nothing about this to anyone; but go, show yourself to the priest and present the offering that Moses commanded, for a testimony [to your healing] and as an evidence to the people.*

---

## Matthew 12:34-37 Amplified Bible, Classic Edition

*34 You offspring of vipers! How can you speak good things when you are evil (wicked)? For out of the fullness (the overflow, the superabundance) of the heart the mouth speaks. 35 The good man from his inner good treasure flings forth good things, and the evil man out of his inner evil storehouse flings forth evil things. 36 But I tell you, on the day of judgment men will have to give account for every idle (inoperative, nonworking) word they speak. 37 For by your words you will be justified and acquitted, and by your words you will be condemned and sentenced.*

---

## Matthew 19:23-26 Amplified Bible, Classic Edition

*23 And Jesus said to His disciples, Truly I say to you, it will be difficult for a rich man to get into the kingdom of heaven. 24 Again I tell you, it is easier for a camel to go through the eye of a needle than for a rich man to go into the kingdom of heaven. 25 When the disciples heard this, they were utterly puzzled (astonished, bewildered), saying, Who then can be saved [from eternal death]? 26 But Jesus looked at them and said, With men this is impossible, but all things are possible with God.*

---

## Matthew 23:23 Amplified Bible, Classic Edition

*23 Woe to you, scribes and Pharisees, pretenders (hypocrites)! For you give a tenth of your mint and dill and cummin and have neglected and omitted the weightier (more important) matters of the Law — right and justice and mercy and fidelity. These you ought [particularly] to have done, without neglecting the others.*

---

## Matthew 25:29   Amplified Bible, Classic Edition

*29 For to everyone who has will more be given, and he will be furnished richly so that he will have an abundance; but from the one who does not have, even what he does have will be taken away.*

---

## Mark

## Mark 4:18-19   Amplified Bible, Classic Edition

*18 And the ones sown among the thorns are others who hear the Word; 19 Then the cares and anxieties of the world and distractions of the age, and the pleasure and delight and false glamour and deceitfulness of riches, and the craving and passionate desire for other things creep in and choke and suffocate the Word, and it becomes fruitless.*

---

## Mark 4:24 Amplified Bible, Classic Edition

*24 And He said to them, Be careful what you are hearing. The measure [of thought and study] you give [to the truth you hear] will be the measure [of virtue and knowledge] that comes back to you — and more [besides] will be given to you who hear.*

---

## Mark 4:26-29 Amplified Bible, Classic Edition

*26 And He said, The kingdom of God is like a man who scatters seed upon the ground, 27 And then continues sleeping and rising night and day while the seed sprouts and grows and increases — he knows not how. 28 The earth produces [acting] by itself — first the blade, then the ear, then the full grain in the ear. 29 But when the grain is ripe and permits, immediately he sends forth [the reapers] and puts in the sickle, because the harvest stands ready.*

---

## Mark 10:29-30 Amplified Bible, Classic Edition

29 *Jesus said, Truly I tell you, there is no one who has given up and left house or brothers or sisters or mother or father or children or lands for My sake and for the Gospel's* 30 *Who will not receive a hundred times as much now in this time — houses and brothers and sisters and mothers and children and lands, with persecutions — and in the age to come, eternal life.*

---

## Mark 11:23-24 Amplified Bible, Classic Edition

23 *Truly I tell you, whoever says to this mountain, Be lifted up and thrown into the sea! and does not doubt at all in his heart but believes that what he says will take place, it will be done for him.* 24 *For this reason I am telling you, whatever you ask for in prayer, believe (trust and be confident) that it is granted to you, and you will [get it].*

---

## Luke

## Luke 4:18-19  Amplified Bible, Classic Edition

*The Spirit of the Lord [is] upon Me, because He has anointed Me [the Anointed One, the Messiah] to preach the good news (the Gospel) to the poor; He has sent Me to announce release to the captives and recovery of sight to the blind, to send forth as delivered those who are oppressed [who are downtrodden, bruised, crushed, and broken down by calamity],* 19 *To proclaim the accepted and acceptable year of the Lord [the day when salvation and the free favors of God profusely abound].*

---

## Luke 6:27-38 Amplified Bible, Classic Edition

27 *But I say to you who are listening now to Me: in order to heed, make it a practice to] love your enemies, treat well (do good to, act nobly toward) those who detest you and pursue you with hatred,*

*[28] Invoke blessings upon and pray for the happiness of those who curse you, implore God's blessing (favor) upon those who abuse you [who revile, reproach, disparage, and high-handedly misuse you]. [29] To the one who strikes you on the jaw or cheek, offer the other jaw or cheek also; and from him who takes away your outer garment, do not withhold your undergarment as well. [30] Give away to everyone who begs of you [who is in want of necessities], and of him who takes away from you your goods, do not demand or require them back again. [31] And as you would like and desire that men would do to you, do exactly so to them. [32] If you [merely] love those who love you, why quality of credit and thanks is that to you? For even the [very] sinners love their lovers (those who love them). [33] And if you are kind and good and do favors to and benefit those who are kind and good and do favors to and benefit you, what[j] quality of credit and thanks is that to you? For even the preeminently sinful do the same. [34] And if you lend money at interest to those from whom you hope to receive, what quality of credit and thanks is that to you? Even notorious sinners lend money at interest to sinners, so as to recover as much again. [35] But love your enemies and be kind and do good [doing favors so that someone derives benefit from them] and lend, expecting and hoping for nothing in return but considering nothing as lost and despairing of no one; and then your recompense (your reward) will be great (rich, strong, intense, and abundant), and you will be sons of the Most High, for He is kind and charitable and good to the ungrateful and the selfish and wicked. [36] So be merciful (sympathetic, tender, responsive, and compassionate) even as your Father is [all these].[37] Judge not [neither pronouncing judgment nor subjecting to censure], and you will not be judged; do not condemn and pronounce guilty, and you will not be condemned and pronounced guilty; acquit and forgive and[j] release (give up resentment, let it drop), and you will be acquitted and forgiven and released. [38] Give, and [gifts] will be given to you; good measure, pressed down, shaken together, and running over, will they pour into [the pouch formed by] the bosom [of your robe and used as a bag]. For with the measure you deal out [with the measure you use when you confer benefits on others], it will be measured back to you.*

## Luke 11:42 New King James Version

42 *"But woe to you Pharisees! For you tithe mint and rue and all manner of herbs and pass by justice and the love of God. These you ought to have done, without leaving the others undone.*

## Luke 12:16-21 Amplified Bible, Classic Edition

16 *Then He told them a parable, saying, The land of a rich man was fertile and yielded plentifully. 17 And he considered and debated within himself, What shall I do? I have no place [in which] to gather together my harvest. 18 And he said, I will do this: I will pull down my storehouses and build larger ones, and there I will store all my grain or produce and my goods. 19 And I will say to my soul, Soul, you have many good things laid up, [enough] for many years. Take your ease; eat, drink, and enjoy yourself merrily. 20 But God said to him, You fool! This very night they [the messengers of God] will demand your soul of you; and all the things that you have prepared, whose will they be? 21 So it is with the one who continues to lay up and hoard possessions for himself and is not rich [in his relation] to God [this is how he fares].*

### Footnotes

*Luke 12:18 Some ancient manuscripts read "grain;" some read "produce" or "fruits."*

*Luke 12:20 Marvin Vincent, Word Studies: "The indefiniteness is impressive."*

## Luke 12:31-32 Amplified Bible, Classic Edition

31 *Only aim at and strive for and seek His kingdom, and all these things shall be supplied to you also. 32 Do not be seized with alarm and struck with fear, little flock, for it is your Father's good*

*pleasure to give you the kingdom!*

---

## Luke 12:48   Amplified Bible, Classic Edition

*48 But he who did not know and did things worthy of a beating shall be beaten with few [lashes]. For everyone to whom much is given, of him shall much be required; and of him to whom men entrust much, they will require and demand all the more.*

---

## Luke 16:9-12 Amplified Bible, Classic Edition

*9 And I tell you, make friends for yourselves by means of unrighteous mammon deceitful riches, money, possessions), so that when it fails, they [those you have favored] may receive and welcome you into the everlasting habitations (dwellings). 10 He who is faithful in a very little [thing] is faithful also in much, and he who is dishonest and unjust in a very little [thing] is dishonest and unjust also in much. 11 Therefore if you have not been faithful in the [case of] unrighteous mammon deceitful riches, money, possessions), who will entrust to you the true riches? 12 And if you have not proved faithful in that which belongs to another [whether God or man], who will give you that which is your own [that is, the true riches]?*

---

## Luke 18:18-25 Amplified Bible, Classic Edition

*18 And a certain ruler asked Him, Good Teacher [You who are essentially and perfectly morally good], what shall I do to inherit eternal life [to partake of eternal salvation in the Messiah's kingdom]? 19 Jesus said to him, Why do you call Me essentially and perfectly morally] good? No one is essentially and perfectly morally] good — except God only. 20 You know the commandments: Do not commit adultery, do not kill, do not steal, do not witness falsely, honor your father and your mother. 21 And he replied, All these I have kept from my youth. 22 And when Jesus heard it, He said to him, One thing you still lack. Sell everything that you have and divide [the money] among the poor, and you will have [rich] treasure in heaven; and come back [and] follow Me [become My disciple, join My party, and accompany Me].* 23 *But when he heard this, he became distressed and very sorrowful, for he was rich—exceedingly so.* 24 *Jesus, observing him, said, How difficult it is for those who have wealth to enter the kingdom of God!* 25 *For it is easier for a camel to enter through a needle's eye than [for] a rich man to enter the kingdom of God.*

---

# John

## John 10:10 Amplified Bible, Classic Edition

10 *The thief comes only in order to steal and kill and destroy. I came that they may have and enjoy life, and have it in abundance (to the full, till it overflows).*

---

## John 14:12-16  Amplified Bible, Classic Edition

12 *I assure you, most solemnly I tell you, if anyone steadfastly believes in Me, he will himself be able to do the things that I do; and he will do even greater things than these, because I go to the Father.* 13 *And I will do [I Myself will grant] whatever you ask in My Name [as presenting all that I Am], so that the Father may be glorified and extolled in (through) the Son.* 14 *[Yes] I will grant [I Myself will do for you] whatever you shall ask in My Name [as presenting all that I Am].* 15 *If you [really] love Me, you will keep (obey) My commands.* 16 *And I will ask the Father, and He will give you another Comforter (Counselor, Helper, Intercessor, Advocate, Strengthener, and Standby), that He may remain with you forever—*

---

# Romans

## Romans 4:16-18   Amplified Bible, Classic Edition

16 *Therefore, [inheriting] the promise is the outcome of faith and depends [entirely] on faith, in order that it might be given as an act of grace (unmerited favor), to make it stable and valid and guaranteed to all his descendants — not only to the devotees and adherents of the Law, but also to those who share the faith of Abraham, who is [thus] the father of us all.* 17 *As it is written, I have made you the father of many nations. [He was appointed our father] in the sight of God in Whom he believed, Who gives life to the dead and speaks of the nonexistent things that [He has foretold and promised] as if they [already] existed.* 18 *[For Abraham, human reason for] hope being gone, hoped in faith that he should become the father of many nations, as he had been promised, So [numberless] shall your descendants be.*

---

## Romans 5:17 Amplified Bible, Classic Edition

17 *For if because of one man's trespass (lapse, offense) death reigned through that one, much more surely will those who receive [God's] overflowing grace (unmerited favor) and the free gift of righteousness [putting them into right standing with Himself] reign as kings in life through the one-Man Jesus Christ (the Messiah, the Anointed One).*

---

## Romans 10:17 Amplified Bible, Classic Edition

17 *So faith comes by hearing [what is told], and what is heard comes by the preaching [of the message that came from the lips] of Christ (the Messiah Himself).*

---

## Romans 12:2 Amplified Bible, Classic Edition

2 *Do not be conformed to this world (this age), [fashioned after and adapted to its external, superficial customs], but be transformed*

*(changed) by the [entire] renewal of your mind [by its new ideals and its new attitude], so that you may prove [for yourselves] what is the good and acceptable and perfect will of God, even the thing which is good and acceptable and perfect [in His sight for you].*

---

## Romans 15:13   Amplified Bible, Classic Edition

*13 May the God of your hope so fill you with all joy and peace in believing [through the experience of your faith] that by the power of the Holy Spirit you may abound and be overflowing (bubbling over) with hope.*

---

## 1 Corinthians

## 1 Corinthians 2:16 Amplified Bible, Classic Edition

*16 For who has known or understood the mind (the counsels and purposes) of the Lord so as to guide and instruct Him and give Him knowledge? But we have the mind of Christ (the Messiah) and do hold the thoughts (feelings and purposes) of His heart.*

---

## 1 Corinthians 3:6   Amplified Bible, Classic Edition

*6 I planted, Apollos watered, but God [all the while] was making it grow and [He] gave the increase.*

---

## 1 Corinthians 3:22 Amplified Bible, Classic Edition

*22 Whether Paul or Apollos or Cephas (Peter), or the universe or life or death, or the immediate and threatening present or the [subsequent and uncertain] future — all are yours,*

---

## 1 Corinthians 9:14 Amplified Bible, Classic Edition

*14 [On the same principle] the Lord directed that those who publish the good news (the Gospel) should live (get their maintenance) by the Gospel.*

---

## 1 Corinthians 9:24   Amplified Bible, Classic Edition

*24 Do you not know that in a race all the runners compete, but [only] one receives the prize? So run [your race] that you may lay hold [of the prize] and make it yours.*

---

## 2 Corinthians

## 2 Corinthians 4:18 Amplified Bible, Classic Edition

*18 Since we consider and look not to the things that are seen but to the things that are unseen; for the things that are visible are temporal (brief and fleeting), but the things that are invisible are deathless and everlasting.*

## 2 Corinthians 5:17   Amplified Bible, Classic Edition

*17 Therefore if any person is [ingrafted] in Christ (the Messiah) he is a new creation (a new creature altogether); the old [previous moral and spiritual condition] has passed away. Behold, the fresh and new has come!*

---

## 2 Corinthians 8:9 Amplified Bible, Classic Edition

*9 For you are becoming progressively acquainted with and recognizing more strongly and clearly the grace of our Lord Jesus Christ (His kindness, His gracious generosity, His undeserved favor and spiritual blessing), [in] that though He was [so very] rich, yet for your sakes He became [so very] poor, in order that by His poverty you might become enriched (abundantly supplied)*

---

## 2 Corinthians 10:5 Amplified Bible, Classic Edition

⁵ *[Inasmuch as we] refute arguments and theories and reasonings and every proud and lofty thing that sets itself up against the [true] knowledge of God; and we lead every thought and purpose away captive into the obedience of Christ (the Messiah, the Anointed One),*

---

## 2 Corinthians 9:6-11 Amplified Bible, Classic Edition

⁶ *[Remember] this: he who sows sparingly and grudgingly will also reap sparingly and grudgingly, and he who sows generously that blessings may come to someone] will also reap generously and with blessings. ⁷ Let each one [give] as he has made up his own mind and purposed in his heart, not reluctantly or sorrowfully or under compulsion, for God loves (He takes pleasure in, prizes above other things, and is unwilling to abandon or to do without) a cheerful (joyous, "prompt to do it") giver [whose heart is in his giving]. ⁸ And God is able to make all grace (every favor and earthly blessing) come to you in abundance, so that you may always and under all circumstances and whatever the need be self-sufficient [possessing enough to require no aid or support and furnished in abundance for every good work and charitable donation]. ⁹ As it is written, He [the benevolent person] scatters abroad; He gives to the poor; His deeds of justice and goodness and kindness and benevolence will go on and endure forever! ¹⁰ And [God] Who provides seed for the sower and bread for eating will also provide and multiply your [resources for] sowing and increase the fruits of your righteousness] which manifests itself in active goodness, kindness, and charity]. ¹¹ Thus you will be enriched in all things and in every way, so that you can be generous, and [your generosity as it is] administered by us will bring forth thanksgiving to God.*

---

## 2 Corinthians chapter 9 New King James Version Administering the Gift

*Now concerning the ministering to the saints, it is superfluous for me to write to you; ²for I know your willingness, about which I boast of you to the Macedonians, that Achaia was ready a year ago; and your zeal has stirred up the majority. ³Yet I have sent the brethren, lest our boasting of you should be in vain in this respect, that, as I said, you may be ready; ⁴lest if some Macedonians come with me and find you unprepared, we (not to mention you!) should be ashamed of this confident boasting. ⁵Therefore I thought it necessary to exhort the brethren to go to you ahead of time, and prepare your generous gift beforehand, which you had previously promised, that it may be ready as a matter of generosity and not as a grudging obligation.*

## The Cheerful Giver

*⁶But this I say: He who sows sparingly will also reap sparingly, and he who sows bountifully will also reap bountifully. ⁷So let each one give as he purposes in his heart, not grudgingly or of necessity; for God loves a cheerful giver. ⁸And God is able to make all grace abound toward you, that you, always having all sufficiency in all things, may have an abundance for every good work. ⁹As it is written: "He has dispersed abroad, He has given to the poor; His righteousness endures forever." ¹⁰Now may He who supplies seed to the sower, and bread for food,ᴶsupply and multiply the seed you have sown and increase the fruits of your righteousness, ¹¹while you are enriched in everything for all liberality, which causes thanksgiving through us to God. ¹²For the administration of this service not only supplies the needs of the saints, but also is abounding through many thanksgivings to God, ¹³while, through the proof of this ministry, they glorify God for the obedience of your confession to the gospel of Christ, and for your liberal sharing with them and all men, ¹⁴and by their prayer for you, who long for you because of the exceeding grace of God in you. ¹⁵Thanks be to God for His indescribable gift!*

---

## Galatians 3:9 Amplified Bible, Classic Edition

*9 So then, those who are people of faith are blessed and made happy and favored by God [as partners in fellowship] with the believing and trusting Abraham.*

---

## Galatians 3:13-14 Amplified Bible, Classic Edition

*13 Christ purchased our freedom [redeeming us] from the curse (doom) of the Law [and its condemnation] by [Himself] becoming a curse for us, for it is written [in the Scriptures], Cursed is everyone who hangs on a tree (is crucified); 14 To the end that through [their receiving] Christ Jesus, the blessing [promised] to Abraham might come upon the Gentiles, so that we through faith might [all] receive [the realization of] the promise of the [Holy] Spirit.*

---

## Galatians 3:29 Amplified Bible, Classic Edition

*29 And if you belong to Christ [are in Him Who is Abraham's Seed], then you are Abraham's offspring and [spiritual] heirs according to promise.*

---

## Galatians 6:7-8 Amplified Bible, Classic Edition

*7 Do not be deceived and deluded and misled; God will not allow Himself to be sneered at (scorned, disdained, or mocked by mere pretensions or professions, or by His precepts being set aside.) [He inevitably deludes himself who attempts to delude God.] For whatever a man sows, that and that only is what he will reap. 8 For he who sows to his own flesh (lower nature, sensuality) will from the flesh reap decay and ruin and destruction, but he who sows to the Spirit will from the Spirit reap eternal life.*

---

## Ephesians

### Ephesians 1:3-4  Amplified Bible, Classic Edition

*³ May blessing (praise, laudation, and eulogy) be to the God and Father of our Lord Jesus Christ (the Messiah) Who has blessed us in Christ with every spiritual (given by the Holy Spirit) blessing in the heavenly realm! ⁴ Even as [in His love] He chose us [actually picked us out for Himself as His own] in Christ before the foundation of the world, that we should be holy (consecrated and set apart for Him) and blameless in His sight, even above reproach, before Him in love.*

---

### Ephesians 2:10 Amplified Bible, Classic Edition

*¹⁰ For we are God's [own] handiwork (His workmanship), recreated in Christ Jesus, [born anew] that we may do those good works which God predestined (planned beforehand) for us [taking paths which He prepared ahead of time], that we should walk in them [living the good life which He prearranged and made ready for us to live].*

### Ephesians 4:28 Amplified Bible, Classic Edition

*²⁸ Let the thief steal no more, but rather let him be industrious, making an honest living with his own hands, so that he may be able to give to those in need.*

---

## Philippians

### Philippians 4:6 Amplified Bible, Classic Edition

*⁶ Do not fret or have any anxiety about anything, but in every circumstance and in everything, by prayer and petition (definite requests), with thanksgiving, continue to make your wants known to God.*

---

## Philippians 4:13 Amplified Bible, Classic Edition

*13 I have strength for all things in Christ Who empowers me [I am ready for anything and equal to anything through Him Who infuses inner strength into me; I am self-sufficient in Christ's sufficiency].*

---

## Philippians 4:17-19 Amplified Bible, Classic Edition

*17 Not that I seek or am eager for [your] gift, but I do seek and am eager for the fruit which increases to your credit [the harvest of blessing that is accumulating to your account]. 18 But I have [your full payment] and more; I have everything I need and am amply supplied, now that I have received from Epaphroditus the gifts you sent me. [They are the] fragrant odor of an offering and sacrifice which God welcomes and in which He delights. 19 And my God will liberally supply fill to the full) your every need according to His riches in glory in Christ Jesus.*

---

## Colossians 3:1-2

## Colossians 3:1-2   Amplified Bible, Classic Edition

*If then you have been raised with Christ [to a new life, thus sharing His resurrection from the dead], aim at and seek the [rich, eternal treasures] that are above, where Christ is, seated at the right hand of God. 2 And set your minds and keep them set on what is above (the higher things), not on the things that are on the earth.*

---

## 2 Thessalonians

## 2 Thessalonians 3:10   Amplified Bible, Classic Edition

*10 For while we were yet with you, we gave you this rule and charge: If anyone will not work, neither let him eat.*

---

## 1 Timothy

### 1 Timothy 4:8 Amplified Bible, Classic Edition

*8 For physical training is of some value (useful for a little), but godliness (spiritual training) is useful and of value in everything and in every way, for it holds promise for the present life and also for the life which is to come.*

---

### 1 Timothy 6:10 Amplified Bible, Classic Edition

*10 For the love of money is a root of all evils; it is through this craving that some have been led astray and have wandered from the faith and pierced themselves through with many acute [mental] pangs.*

---

### 1 Timothy 6:17-19 Amplified Bible, Classic Edition

*17 As for the rich in this world, charge them not to be proud and arrogant and contemptuous of others, nor to set their hopes on uncertain riches, but on God, Who richly and ceaselessly provides us with everything for [our] enjoyment. 18 [Charge them] to do good, to be rich in good works, to be liberal and generous of heart, ready to share [with others], 19 In this way laying up for themselves [the riches that endure forever as] a good foundation for the future, so that they may grasp that which is life indeed.*

---

## 2 Timothy

### 2 Timothy 1:7 Amplified Bible, Classic Edition

*7 For God did not give us a spirit of timidity (of cowardice, of craven and cringing and fawning fear), but [He has given us a spirit] of power and of love and of calm and well-balanced mind and discipline and self-control.*

## Hebrews

### Hebrews 7:2 Amplified Bible, Classic Edition

*2 And Abraham gave to him a tenth portion of all [the spoil]. He is primarily, as his name when translated indicates, king of righteousness, and then he is also king of Salem, which means king of peace.*

### Hebrews 7:5 Amplified Bible, Classic Edition

*5 And it is true that those descendants of Levi who are charged with the priestly office are commanded in the Law to take tithes from the people — which means, from their brethren — though these have descended from Abraham.*

### Hebrews 7:8 Amplified Bible, Classic Edition

*8 Furthermore, here [in the Levitical priesthood] tithes are received by men who are subject to death; while there [in the case of Melchizedek], they are received by one of whom it is testified that he lives [perpetuall].*

### Hebrews 7:1-10 Amplified Bible, Classic Edition

*For this Melchizedek, king of Salem [and] priest of the Most High God, met Abraham as he returned from the slaughter of the kings and blessed him, 2 And Abraham gave to him a tenth portion of all [the spoil]. He is primarily, as his name when translated indicates, king of righteousness, and then he is also king of Salem, which means king of peace. 3 Without [record of] father or mother or ancestral line, neither with beginning of days nor ending of life, but, resembling the Son of God, he continues to be a priest without interruption and without successor. 4 Now observe and consider how great [a personage] this was to whom even Abraham the patriarch gave a tenth [the topmost or the pick of the heap] of the spoils. 5 And it is true that those descendants of Levi who are charged with the priestly office are commanded in the Law to take tithes from the people — which means, from their brethren — though these have descended from Abraham. ⁶ But this person who has not their Levitical ancestry received tithes from Abraham [himself] and blessed him who possessed the promises [of God]. ⁷ Yet it is beyond all contradiction that it is the lesser person who is blessed by the greater one. ⁸ Furthermore, here [in the Levitical priesthood] tithes are received by men who are subject to death; while there [in the case of Melchizedek], they are received by one of whom it is testified that he lives [perpetually]. ⁹ A person might even say that Levi [the father of the priestly tribe] himself, who received tithes (the tenth), paid tithes through Abraham, ¹⁰ For he was still in the loins of his forefather [Abraham] when Melchizedek met him [Abraham].*

---

## Hebews

## Hebrews 11:3   Amplified Bible, Classic Edition

*³ By faith we understand that the worlds [during the successive ages] were framed (fashioned, put in order, and equipped for their intended purpose) by the word of God, so that what we see was not made out of things which are visible.*

---

## James_

## James 1:5-8 Amplified Bible, Classic Edition

*⁵ If any of you is deficient in wisdom, let him ask of the giving God [Who gives] to everyone liberally and ungrudgingly, without reproaching or faultfinding, and it will be given him. ⁶ Only it must be in faith that he asks with no wavering (no hesitating, no doubting). For the one who wavers (hesitates, doubts) is like the billowing surge out at sea that is blown hither and thither and tossed by the wind. ⁷ For truly, let not such a person imagine that he will receive anything [he asks for] from the Lord, ⁸ [For being as he is] a man of two minds (hesitating, dubious, irresolute), [he is] unstable and unreliable and uncertain about everything [he thinks, feels, decides].*

### James 1:17 Amplified Bible, Classic Edition

*17 Every good gift and every perfect free, large, full) gift is from above; it comes down from the Father of all [that gives] light, in [the shining of] Whom there can be no variation [rising or setting] or shadow cast by His turning [as in an eclipse].*

### James 2:17 Amplified Bible, Classic Edition

*17 So also faith, if it does not have works (deeds and actions of obedience to back it up), by itself is destitute of power (inoperative, dead).*

### James 3:16-18  Amplified Bible, Classic Edition

*For wherever there is jealousy (envy) and contention (rivalry and selfish ambition), there will also be confusion (unrest, disharmony, rebellion) and all sorts of evil and vile practices. 17 But the wisdom from above is first of all pure (undefiled); then it is peace-loving, courteous (considerate, gentle). [It is willing to] yield to reason, full of compassion and good fruits; it is wholehearted and straightforward, impartial and unfeigned (free from doubts, wavering, and insincerity). 18 And the harvest of righteousness (of conformity to God's will in thought and deed) is [the fruit of the seed] sown in peace by those who work for and make peace [in themselves and in others, that peace which means concord, agreement, and harmony between individuals, with undisturbedness, in a peaceful mind free from fears and agitating passions and moral conflicts].*

### James 4:2 Amplified Bible, Classic Edition

*2 You are jealous and covet [what others have] and your desires go unfulfilled; [so] you become murderers. [To hate is to murder as far as your hearts are concerned.] You burn with envy and anger and are not able to obtain [the gratification, the contentment, and the happiness that you seek], so you fight and war. You do not have, because you do not ask.*

**CEV**

*You want something you don't have, and you will do anything to get it. You will even kill! But you still cannot get what you want, and you won't get it by fighting and arguing. You should pray for it.*

*EASY*

*You want to have something for yourself, but you do not get what you want. You even kill other people. You try to take things that are not yours. But you cannot get them. So you fight and you quarrel with each other. But you do not have these things because you do not ask God for them.*

*PHILLIPS*

*But about the feuds and struggles that exist among you — where do you suppose they come from? Can't you see that they arise from conflicting passions within yourselves? You crave for something and don't get it, you are jealous and envious of what others have got and you don't possess it yourselves. Consequently in your exasperated frustration you struggle and fight with one another. You don't get what you want because you don't ask God for it. And when you do ask he doesn't give it to you, for you ask in quite the wrong spirit — you only want to satisfy your own desires.*

---

**James 4:7  Amplified Bible, Classic Edition**

*7 So be subject to God. Resist the devil [stand firm against him], and he will flee from you.*

*7-10 So let God work his will in you. Yell a loud no to the Devil and watch him make himself scarce. Say a quiet yes to God and he'll be there in no time. Quit dabbling in sin. Purify your inner life. Quit playing the field. Hit bottom, and cry your eyes out. The fun and games are over. Get serious, really serious. Get down on your knees before the Master; it's the only way you'll get on your feet.*

---

## James 4:8 Amplified Bible, Classic Edition

*8 Come close to God and He will come close to you. [Recognize that you are] sinners, get your soiled hands clean; [realize that you have been disloyal] wavering individuals with divided interests, and purify your hearts [of your spiritual adultery].*

---

## 1 Peter

## 1 Peter 1:25 Amplified Bible, Classic Edition

*25 But the Word of the Lord divine instruction, the Gospel) endures forever. And this Word is the good news which was preached to you.*

---

## 1 Peter 5:7 Amplified Bible, Classic Edition

*7 Casting the whole of your care [all your anxieties, all your worries, all your concerns, once and for all] on Him, for He cares for you affectionately and cares about you watchfully.*

---

## 1 John

## 1 John 2:26-27  Amplified Bible, Classic Edition

*26 I write this to you with reference to those who would deceive you [seduce and lead you astray]. 27 But as for you, the anointing (the sacred appointment, the unction) which you received from Him abides [permanently] in you; [so] then you have no need that anyone should instruct you. But just as His anointing teaches you concerning everything and is true and is no falsehood, so you must abide in (live in, never depart from) Him [being rooted in Him, knit to Him], just as [His anointing] has taught you [to do].*

---

## John 5:4-5   Amplified Bible, Classic Edition

*4 For whatever is born of God is victorious over the world; and this is the victory that conquers the world, even our faith. 5 Who is it that is victorious over [that conquers] the world but he who believes that Jesus is the Son of God [who adheres to, trusts in, and relies on that fact]?*

---

## John 5:18-21   Amplified Bible, Classic Edition

*18 We know [absolutely] that anyone born of God does not [deliberately and knowingly] practice committing sin, but the One Who was begotten of God carefully watches over and protects him [Christ's divine presence within him preserves him against the evil], and the wicked one does not lay hold (get a grip) on him or touch [him]. 19 We know [positively] that we are of God, and the whole world [around us] is under the power of the evil one. 20 And we [have seen and] know [positively] that the Son of God has [actually] come to this world and has given us understanding and insight [progressively] to perceive (recognize) and come to know better and more clearly Him Who is true; and we are in Him Who is true – in His Son Jesus Christ (the Messiah). This [Man] is the true God and Life eternal. 21 Little children, keep yourselves from idols (false gods) – [from anything and everything that would occupy the place in your heart due to God, from any sort of substitute for Him that would take first place in your life]. Amen (so let it be).*

---

## 3 John

### 3 John 1-8 Amplified Bible, Classic Edition

*¹ The elderly elder [of the church addresses this letter] to the beloved (esteemed) Gaius, whom I truly love. ² Beloved, I pray that you may prosper in every way and [that your body] may keep well, even as [I know] your soul keeps well and prospers. ³ In fact, I greatly rejoiced when [some of] the brethren from time to time arrived and spoke [so highly] of the sincerity and fidelity of your life, as indeed you do live in the Truth [the whole Gospel presents]. ⁴ I have no greater joy than this, to hear that my [spiritual] children are living their lives in the Truth. ⁵ Beloved, it is a fine and faithful work that you are doing when you give any service to the [Christian] brethren, and [especially when they are] strangers. ⁶ They have testified before the church of your love and friendship. You will do well to forward them on their journey [and you will please do so] in a way worthy of God's [service]. ⁷ For these [traveling missionaries] have gone out for the Name's sake (for His sake) and are accepting nothing from the Gentiles (the heathen, the non-Israelites). ⁸ So we ourselves ought to support such people [to welcome and provide for them], in order that we may be fellow workers in the Truth (the whole Gospel) and cooperate with its teachers.*

---

## Revelation

### Revelation 1:5-6 Amplified Bible, Classic Edition

*⁵ And from Jesus Christ the faithful and trustworthy Witness, the Firstborn of the dead [first to be brought back to life] and the Prince (Ruler) of the kings of the earth. To Him Who ever loves us and has once [for all] loosed and freed us from our sins by His own blood, ⁶ And formed us into a kingdom (a royal race), priests to His God and Father — to Him be the glory and the power and the majesty and the dominion throughout the ages and forever and ever. Amen (so be it).*

---

## Revelation 5:10 Amplified Bible, Classic Edition

[10] *And You have made them a kingdom (royal race) and priests to our God, and they shall reign [as kings] over the earth!*

---

# Bible Scripture Sources

21st Century King James Version **(KJ21)** Copyright © 1994 by Deuel Enterprises, Inc.; American Standard Version **(ASV)** Public Domain (Why are modern Bible translations copyrighted?); Amplified Bible **(AMP)** Copyright © 2015 by The Lockman Foundation, La Habra, CA 90631. All rights reserved.; Amplified Bible, Classic Edition **(AMPC)** Copyright © 1954, 1958, 1962, 1964, 1965, 1987 by The Lockman Foundation; BRG Bible **(BRG)** Blue Red and Gold Letter Edition™ Copyright © 2012 BRG Bible Ministries. Used by Permission. All rights reserved. BRG Bible is a Registered Trademark in U.S. Patent and Trademark Office #4145648; Christian Standard Bible **(CSB)** The Christian Standard Bible. Copyright © 2017 by Holman Bible Publishers. Used by permission. Christian Standard Bible®, and CSB® are federally registered trademarks of Holman Bible Publishers, all rights reserved. ; Common English Bible **(CEB)** Copyright © 2011 by Common English Bible; Complete Jewish Bible **(CJB)** Copyright © 1998 by David H. Stern. All rights reserved. ; Contemporary English Version **(CEV)** Copyright © 1995 by American Bible Society For more information about CEV, visit www.bibles.com and www.cev.bible.; Darby Translation **(DARBY)** Public Domain (Why are modern Bible translations copyrighted?); Douay-Rheims 1899 American Edition **(DRA)** Public Domain (Why are modern Bible translations copyrighted?); Easy-to-Read Version **(ERV)** Copyright © 2006 by Bible League International; EasyEnglish Bible **(EASY)** Easy English Bible Copyright © Mission Assist 2019 - Charitable Incorporated Organization 1162807. Used by permission. All rights reserved.; Evangelical Heritage Version **(EHV)** The Holy Bible, Evangelical Heritage Version®, EHV®, © 2019 Wartburg Project, Inc. All rights reserved.; English Standard

Version **(ESV)** The Holy Bible, English Standard Version. ESV® Text Edition: 2016. Copyright © 2001 by Crossway Bibles, a publishing ministry of Good News Publishers.; English Standard Version Anglicised **(ESVUK)** The Holy Bible, English Standard Version Copyright © 2001 by Crossway Bibles, a division of Good News Publishers.; Expanded Bible **(EXB)** The Expanded Bible, Copyright © 2011 Thomas Nelson Inc. All rights reserved. ; 1599 Geneva Bible **(GNV)** Geneva Bible, 1599 Edition. Published by Tolle Lege Press. All rights reserved. No part of this publication may be reproduced or transmitted in any form or by any means, electronic or mechanical, without written permission from the publisher, except in the case of brief quotations in articles, reviews, and broadcasts. ; GOD'S WORD Translation **(GW)** Copyright © 1995, 2003, 2013, 2014, 2019, 2020 by God's Word to the Nations Mission Society. All rights reserved.; Good News Translation **(GNT)** Good News Translation® (Today's English Version, Second Edition) © 1992 American Bible Society. All rights reserved. For more information about GNT, visit www.bibles.com and www.gnt.bible.; Holman Christian Standard Bible **(HCSB)** Copyright © 1999, 2000, 2002, 2003, 2009 by Holman Bible Publishers, Nashville Tennessee. All rights reserved.; International Children's Bible **(ICB)** The Holy Bible, International Children's Bible® Copyright© 1986, 1988, 1999, 2015 by Thomas Nelson. Used by permission.; International Standard Version **(ISV)** Copyright © 1995-2014 by ISV Foundation. ALL RIGHTS RESERVED INTERNATIONALLY. Used by permission of Davidson Press, LLC.; Jubilee Bible 2000 **(JUB)** Copyright © 2013, 2020 by Ransom Press International ; King James Version **(KJV)** Public Domain; Authorized (King James) Version **(AKJV)** KJV reproduced by permission of Cambridge University Press, the Crown's patentee in the UK.; Legacy Standard Bible **(LSB)** Legacy Standard Bible Copyright ©2021 by The

Lockman Foundation. All rights reserved. Managed in partnership with Three Sixteen Publishing Inc. LSBible.org For Permission to Quote Information visit https://www.LSBible.org.; Lexham English Bible **(LEB)** 2012 by Logos Bible Software. Lexham is a registered trademark of Logos Bible Software; Living Bible **(TLB)** The Living Bible copyright © 1971 by Tyndale House Foundation. Used by permission of Tyndale House Publishers Inc., Carol Stream, Illinois 60188. All rights reserved.; The Message **(MSG)** Copyright © 1993, 2002, 2018 by Eugene H. Peterson; Modern English Version **(MEV)** The Holy Bible, Modern English Version. Copyright © 2014 by Military Bible Association. Published and distributed by Charisma House. ; Names of God Bible **(NOG)** The Names of God Bible (without notes) © 2011 by Baker Publishing Group. ; New American Bible (Revised Edition) **(NABRE)** Scripture texts, prefaces, introductions, footnotes and cross references used in this work are taken from the New American Bible, revised edition © 2010, 1991, 1986, 1970 Confraternity of Christian Doctrine, Inc., Washington, DC All Rights Reserved. No part of this work may be reproduced or transmitted in any form or by any means, electronic or mechanical, including photocopying, recording, or by any information storage and retrieval system, without permission in writing from the copyright owner. ; New American Standard Bible **(NASB)** New American Standard Bible®, Copyright © 1960, 1971, 1977, 1995, 2020 by The Lockman Foundation. All rights reserved.; New American Standard Bible 1995 **(NASB1995)** New American Standard Bible®, Copyright © 1960, 1971, 1977, 1995 by The Lockman Foundation. All rights reserved.; New Catholic Bible **(NCB)** Copyright © 2019 by Catholic Book Publishing Corp. All rights reserved.; New Century Version **(NCV)** The Holy Bible, New Century Version®. Copyright © 2005 by Thomas Nelson, Inc.; New English Translation **(NET)** NET Bible® copyright ©1996-2017 by Biblical Studies Press, L.L.C.